BUILDING UNSTOPPABLE SELF-CONFIDENCE FOR TEENS 2.0 - THE WORKBOOK

MASTER THE FAIL-SAFE FORMULA TO GROW STRONGER, BOLDER, AND MORE UNSTOPPABLE

DEREK T FREEMAN

TABLE OF CONTENTS

INTRODUCTION: INTO THE DARK

Do you want to know a big secret? *You already have self-confidence.* It's true - you were born with it. Unfortunately for many of us, by the time we hit our teens, that confidence gets pushed down and covered up.

But before we get into the juicy details of this "secret," I think it's essential for you to learn a little bit about *me*.

I didn't have a bad childhood. My childhood was probably a lot better than the majority of young people, which makes me both grateful and sad at the same time. I have wonderful parents, and the first 12 years of my life were pretty average. In elementary school, I wasn't the most popular. But I also wasn't picked on. I guess you could say I was "comfortable."

After sixth grade ended, my parents dropped a bomb on my younger brother and me. "We're moving," they told us. "We've found a better house with a better school system. This is going to be a good thing!" I remember being caught off guard, and instantly a flood of concerns came rushing in: "What about my friends? What about my *best* friend?" "I'm going to have to start from scratch." "What if the new people don't like me? What if I don't like them? What if everybody has their own group already, and I don't fit into *any* of them?"

At 13, this scope of reality *was* my life - friends, school, teachers, and parents. And all of that was about to change. Aside from family, every other constant in my life would soon be pulled from beneath me. Luckily, my cousin (who was my age) would join the same school system as me. "I'll have at least *one* friend," I thought. "Maybe that will give me enough time to feel comfortable, and soon enough, I'll be able to find more friends." Well, he ended up sticking it out for about two months. The bullying was so intense that his parents decided to pull him out and homeschool him.

My biggest fear had come to life. I remember dreading *every. single. day.* I hated waking up in the morning; I hated getting on the bus. I feared every march down every hallway. I was unhappy with the way I looked and was paranoid that others were always laughing at me. I still have fond memories of one kid kicking me in the shin as hard as he could every time I walked to my locker. (He didn't like it when I loaded my backpack with books and started using it to shield my leg, however! And ironically, he turned out to be a close friend in high school.) "Why doesn't anyone like me?" was all that ran through my head daily. And after asking myself this question way too many times, I got down to the real question: "Why don't I like *myself*?"

Before you feel too sorry for me, you should know that things ended up pretty great. Yes, middle school and a good amount of high school were unbearable at times, even torturous. But eventually, I did find friends. Some of my friends from high school remain my best friends today. I did well in school, and right after graduating, I toured the country for many years with my band. We played in front of hundreds of thousands of people and put out about six albums - doing things that most never even dream of. Soon after that, my son was born, and I helped run a famous little restaurant for 13+ years. I experienced the birth of my two daughters, built a home studio, and recorded more albums for myself and other artists. I am now happily married, with the best wife, kids, and cats I could ask for - and writing this book!

So why is this important? Why should my life matter to YOU?

First and foremost, I want you to know that I am a *real person* - that I struggled for many years with self-esteem, bullying, and fitting in. And that you are most definitely not alone. Although your life and experiences are specific to you, countless others have (or have had) similar or *worse* stories to tell throughout these early years. Just think about it - there's SO much going on. Teenagers are in a stage of identifying themselves, dealing with new and crazy feelings, and learning tons of "stuff." It's almost impossible not to compare yourself with others while constantly bombarded by outside influences. On top of that, you're expected to choose a career path, learn independence and responsibility, and, oh yeah - make sense of a rapidly changing body. I would honestly be more shocked if these years *weren't* tricky.

But secondly (ok, maybe THIS is foremost) - I need you to understand that you can avoid SO many painful life lessons in the future if you learn to reclaim and build your self-confidence *now*. Read that again! If you're not so satisfied with your life story, or even if you are - know that it can get better. And it WILL. Your gender, race, genetics, family history, and social status do not matter. You will overcome who you *were* and improve and create your entire reality. You will fall in love with who you *are* and become a magnet for amazing things - attracting the people, situations, and circumstances of your dreams. Best of all, you will do it **your** way.

SO HERE'S THE PLAN

It's crucial to me that I don't come across as "preachy." As a teen and even into my 20s, I was very turned off by people who tried to tell me how to feel or what to do. Instead of lecturing, I would like to share the secrets I've discovered over the years, which have transformed me immensely. Feel free to read this book with an open mind and use the suggestions naturally. What works for you? Maybe you read a chapter a day and let it all sink in. Perhaps you read the whole book in one shot and then read it again! Whatever you do, make it enjoyable for yourself.

Also, if you're anything like I was, you're not looking for more work to pile onto your existing workload (and if you are, well, I guess you're ahead of the game). Just know this: the amount of effort you put *into* it is proportional to what you will get *out* of it. So, the end of each chapter will contain reflection points which I've called "Create Your Life." These will be your forks in the road - junctures where you can look inside, exercise your power of decision, and create real change. You can use these moments to begin shaping your life's entire course. I would suggest pondering them first thing in the morning and last thing at night (at minimum) when it's quiet, and you can zone in and focus. Ultimately, this is a self-reflection book - because it's only from *genuine* self-reflection that we can begin to make the changes we wish to see in our lives.

What follows is a transformative formula that quite literally works from the inside out. Over the next nine chapters, you will learn that reconstructing yourself on the inside will result in magical experiences on the outside with a bit of patience.

Yes, there are secrets to life - things I only wish I had known back then. You have so much more power than you realize at this age. So do the internal "work," knowing it's the best investment you'll ever make - not just right now, but for the rest of your life. Never forget - it's FOR you. And no one else can do it. You got this. I'm quite - *confident* in that :)

WELCOME TO THE WORKBOOK

Me again!

If you're reading this, you've got the updated workbook version. You're ready to take your confidence to the next level—and that's something to be proud of.

This version was created to enhance everything you read in the book and directly apply it to your life. Learning is great, but *doing* is where magic happens.

What you will find at the end of each chapter are practical prompts, creative challenges, and reflection points designed to help you dig deep, build yourself up, and take real steps toward the life you **want**. It's like having a personal guide through the confidence-building process—with plenty of space to be honest, messy, and real.

You don't have to do everything perfectly. You just have to show up for yourself.

HERE'S HOW TO GET THE MOST OUT OF THE WORKBOOK:

- **Take your time.** There's no rush. It isn't a test—it's a journey.
- **Write it out.** Putting thoughts on paper can spark real change, even if it feels uncomfortable at first.
- **Be honest.** This workbook is for you. No one else is grading it or reading it (unless you want them to).

- **Revisit pages.** Some exercises might hit differently the second or third time through. That's totally normal.
- **Have fun with it.** Confidence doesn't have to be all serious—it can be creative, playful, and even weird sometimes.

I wrote my original book in a specific order for a reason, however, there's not a "wrong" way to use the workbook. Start at the beginning and work your way through, or flip to the sections that speak to you most. Skip around, scribble in the margins, take breaks, and come back when you're ready. This is your space!

Most importantly? Be patient with yourself. Growth doesn't happen overnight, but every time you open this back up and do the work, you're choosing progress—and that's how confidence is built: one small, brave move at a time.

You can do it. I believe in you, and I can't wait to see what you discover.

—Derek

I PROMISE, YOU'RE IN THERE

Olivia was a well-mannered, quiet student. She was a talented choir singer, but that wasn't considered very cool. Her two best friends sang in the choir too, but Olivia shined. Although her friends encouraged her, Olivia found herself torn between doing something she was passionate about and wanting to be more popular.

On Monday morning at the start of the school year, when getting off the bus, Olivia saw a group of girls on the other end of the parking lot. She knew these girls as the most notorious in the school - the ones *everyone* else wanted to be like. In the past, Olivia had always been too shy to approach them, despite craving their approval. She knew (or thought) they were too far out of her league.

She spied from a distance. The four girls appeared to be picking on one of her friends, Jenna - calling her names and making fun of her (for singing in the choir, probably). Walking closer now, Olivia knew she should do something - but didn't know what. Her heart began to race as the others noticed her, and slowly she became frozen in fear...

Of course, Olivia didn't want to see her friend getting picked on! They grew up together; their parents were friends, and she had known Jenna almost her whole life. But now, for some reason, Olivia was unable to say or do anything. She didn't want the popular girls to think she was weird or different. So when one of the girls yelled, "Liv, you're not friends with Jenna anymore, right??" Olivia told herself it would be easier to join in on the bullying instead of standing up for her friend.

Olivia went on to do something very out of character. She walked right over to the girls and started making fun of Jenna alongside them. She laughed at all of their jokes and agreed with everything they said. "I don't sing anymore, actually," she lied. "That was so last year!" Her friend looked so sad and alone, and Olivia secretly felt terrible inside. She knew she was doing the wrong thing, but she couldn't bring herself to stop.

The more Olivia laughed and joked with the popular girls, the worse she felt about herself. But she was stuck! "Is this what it takes to be popular? Do these girls feel bad about themselves too?" Either way, she continued. The feeling that the cool girls liked her was enough to keep her doing something that felt utterly rotten. She didn't know it yet, but this was a moment that would haunt her.

As time passed, Olivia gradually became a different person - someone unrecognizable. She started wearing clothes that didn't suit her and using language that degraded her. She even began to make fun of her *other* friends behind their backs and tease kids she didn't know. The only thing that made her feel good now was knowing she was part of this new group.

Eventually, Olivia realized that this wasn't what she wanted. Being around those girls turned her into someone she didn't recognize, someone she didn't *like*. She missed being herself and hanging out with her old friends. But it was too late to go back to them. They wanted nothing to do with her. And over the next couple of years, as Olivia "outgrew" the immaturity of the popular girls, she found herself in a place of complete emptiness and regret.

She lost her best friends, behaved in ways she was ashamed of, and essentially went *backward* in life - all because she didn't know her values, worth, strength, or **self**.

THE SEARCH FOR IDENTITY

It's no secret that the teenage years can be difficult.

For many, it's a time of embarrassment and self-doubt as they try to figure out who they are and where they fit in. The constant pressure to conform and meet expectations can make this process even more difficult. The story of Olivia perfectly conveys why **finding yourself** needs to be the first step in building true self-confidence (and making your best decisions!). Unfortunately, many teens give up their search for identity early on simply because it's too hard or seems too daunting. This is a giant mistake - without a strong sense of self, it's really very difficult to achieve anything else.

Simply put, until you *know* yourself, you can't *be* yourself. You'll always try to live up to someone else's expectations instead of your own. And that's just a recipe for unhappiness and frustration.

Think about it – how can you be content when you're always worried about what other people think of you? How can you be your best self when constantly trying to be someone else? When you know who you are and what you stand for, you can start to make decisions based on what's best for YOU. You can be authentic and genuine instead of pretending to be someone you're not.

Knowing yourself will be the basis for all of your decision-making going forward. I'm sure you know that "Plinko" game where the little puck falls, bouncing left or right off of all the little pegs? Well, think of those pegs as the decisions you'll make. If you genuinely know who you are, you'll be able to make decisions that will benefit you, and over the course of many choices, your "puck" will land right where you want it - in a perfect place.

This is an overused slogan, but life doesn't come with an instruction manual. In our early childhood, our parents guide us every step of the way. But what about as we transition into adults? Eventually, you'll have to figure out how to navigate for yourself, and your teen years are the perfect time to start thinking about that. By picking up this book, taking action, and acknowledging this - you are already putting yourself in a better position.

So how do you go about discovering who you are? Well, there's not really a "one size fits all" answer. The answer is as unique as you! That said, we can begin the process by following these steps:

1. **Start *being* yourself.** This seems obvious, but it's less common than you may think. Many teens try to conform to societal norms, even if it's not who they are inside. Don't be afraid to be different and express yourself honestly. Slowly start challenging yourself in this way, little by little, asking yourself, "What would *I* do?"
2. **Find your passion.** We will explore this topic in depth in chapter five. When you're passionate about something, it shows in everything you do. Finding something that excites you and pursuing it can do wonders for self-discovery.
3. **Be open to change.** The world is constantly changing, so you need to become comfortable with adapting. Learn not to be rigid - don't cling too tightly to your past or preconceived notions of who you are. Be willing to grow and readjust as you journey to find the REAL you.

4. **Talk to others.** Ask them about their passions, fears, and dreams for the future. Pay attention to their answers. Be curious as to what makes other people "tick." You may be surprised by what you learn about *yourself*.

5. **Be patient.** Remember, this is a journey, not a destination. There's no need to rush. Allow for quiet time; let the "thinking" take a break and learn to sit with yourself. Enjoy the process. After all - life is meant to be lived, not just figured out!

Of course, the search for identity is not always an easy one. It can be challenging to sort through all the outside noise and distractions and figure out what's important to you. It might be a lot to take in right now, especially if you've never thought about soul searching before. As I mentioned earlier (and this is a remedy for *many* problems) - simply being **aware** that you need to know yourself is half the battle.

It's time to start making yourself a priority internally. Soon you will discover all of the incredible facets of your personality that you never even knew were there. Once you find that core sense of self, nothing can shake you. True freedom is living from your authentic self without worrying about what anyone else thinks. And that is definitely worth the challenge.

THE CHALLENGE OF LABELS

Teenagers face constant pressure to fit into specific categories or "labels." Fitting into these categories is often easier than being fully authentic. This can be a major obstacle in self-discovery because it simply **doesn't tell the whole story**. It's like a quick fix for finding yourself; a "false" identity. Well, the quick fix 99% of the time is not the best fix, or even close. It's like slapping on a "HELLO, my name is (*insert label*)" sticker and calling it a day. It is important to remember that these labels are often limiting and tend to stunt your growth as an individual.

Some "labels" teens might find they attach themselves to include: popular, jock, nerd, goth, punk, or jokester. Overachiever, underachiever, loner, or outcast. Even labels that *feel* like they must be accurate - athlete, musician, artist, writer, dancer, or singer - should not be *defining* you. They are only a tiny portion of the much greater whole - the vast YOU.

Since labels don't tell the whole story, they can easily (and sneakily) prevent us from discovering our true potential. If your label is your full scope of "you," what reason do you have to step outside of it? What reason do you have to grow, explore, or improve?

On top of this, we're often not the "best" at whatever the label represents. For example, if we label ourselves as "jocks," but we're not the best athletes, we might feel like we're not good enough. If you label yourself a "singer," how will you feel when there's a better singer than you? How will it affect you when you lose your voice and *can't* sing? In these cases, doubt and insecurity creep in, blocking us from moving forward and further keeping us from discovering our amazingness. That one hobby or activity doesn't have to be your life. It is a part of who you are, but it doesn't need to be the ruling factor.

Finally, these labels can be pretty restrictive. We may need to behave a certain way or do a specific thing to fit *into* the label. This concept is so misguided! As you'll learn, we can be whoever we want to be and do whatever we want to do. The ultimate goal in finding yourself is to explore your infinite potential!

In the case of Olivia, she so desperately wanted to wear the "popular" label that she began to identify with it. It caused her to be someone she wasn't, and she learned that living under false pretenses never ends well. Labels cause us to get so wrapped up in trying to be someone else that we forget just to be *ourselves*. So regarding labels, remember 1) The label doesn't tell the whole story. 2) The label isn't the only thing that defines you. 3) You are free to explore your potential. 4) You are free to be yourself. Don't ever let **any** outside source dictate who you should be.

ESCAPING THE COMPARATIVE TRAP

A massive side effect of labels is falling prey to the comparative trap, in which you measure everything you do to someone else. We often see it on social media, where people constantly post about their latest accomplishments and "perfect" lives. This is another significant obstacle in self-discovery because it can lead to much self-judgment. It creates pressure, especially for teens, who may feel they need perfect grades, popularity, and many friends to be considered successful.

The problem with this way of thinking is based on the false premise that there is only *one* right way to be. Obviously, this couldn't be further from the truth. Everyone is different and has a unique path to follow. Like Oscar Wilde said beautifully, "Be yourself; everyone else is already taken." By constantly comparing yourself to others, you're setting yourself up for disappointment and missing out on the opportunity to focus on *your* journey.

Many remarkable people prove this point. In fact, history tends ONLY to celebrate the unique ones! The ones who forged a path of their own always did things a little differently; typically, that's why they succeeded.

One example is Oprah Winfrey. She dropped out of college and started work as a news reporter, which was a highly unusual career choice for a woman then. When starting her talk show, she avoided current, popular topic trends and consciously decided to do what felt right to *her*. As a result, she became one of the most successful talk show hosts in history and built an empire worth billions of dollars.

Another great example is Steve Jobs. Jobs was known for relying on his instinct. Although he was fired from his *own company*, he never gave up – he just got more creative. Eventually, Apple hired him back in hopes that he could turn the company around (now one of the biggest tech companies in the world). He was famously revered for his unique way of thinking and for not following the status quo.

The bottom line is that **there is no one right way to be**. Shift your attention to developing and following YOUR voice and uniqueness, which is where the true power is. To help avoid the comparative trap:

1. **Be aware of your thoughts and feelings.** If you constantly compare yourself to others, take a step back and ask why. What are you trying to achieve? What are you trying to prove? Examine your beliefs and question why you feel inferior.
2. **Accept yourself for who you are.** This doesn't mean that you can't strive to improve or be the best you can be, but it does mean that you need to be okay with where you are right now.
3. **Focus on your own journey.** As tempting as it might be, don't try to live up to someone else's standards. Focus on what makes you happy and what you want to achieve in life. Develop your own set of values and stick to them.
4. **Seek positive role models.** Find people in your life who inspire you and make you feel good about yourself. These people can help provide guidance and support as you discover your path.

WHY SELF-ESTEEM MATTERS (YOU ARE WORTHY OF THE BEST)

It may be important to understand the difference between self-esteem and self-confidence. Self-esteem is a broader term; it's how you *feel* about yourself. On the other hand, self-confidence refers to your *trust* in your abilities: in specific tasks, qualities, or judgment calls. A little bit confusing, but think of self-esteem as the foundation for developing self-confidence.

When it comes to having any semblance of a good life, self-esteem is essential. Having high self-esteem means believing you're worthy of the best. It doesn't mean that you're conceited, perfect, or that you don't make mistakes - it means that you have a **healthy** sense of self-worth. You're not going to be afraid to stand up for yourself; you feel good about yourself and your accomplishments, no matter how big or small they may be. Again, high self-esteem works hand in hand with self-confidence because it allows you to take risks and reach your full potential.

"Everything in the universe wants to be loved and accepted. Our personal work is to find the love and acceptance within ourselves."

— SHAKTI GAWAIN

You are worthy because you are alive. You're here - you are a life force. You can think, breathe, create and be aware of it all. You are so dynamic that everything you do has a butterfly effect not only on your life but the lives of others. That isn't meant to scare you or cause you to overthink but rather to empower you! To help you understand that you are *essential.*

Being a teenager puts you in a unique position to make a difference in the world. You have the energy, enthusiasm, and creativity that can change the course of history. You are still learning and growing, which means that you have the potential to be anything you want to be. With the right attitude and support system, you can literally accomplish anything you set your mind to. You are indeed the future.

Yes, your quality of self-esteem will have far-reaching effects all through adulthood, so we're going to make sure it starts strong *now*. As you read, you will continue to learn how to build great self-esteem - and, eventually, unstoppable self-confidence. But you do have to apply the things you learn. That being said, I challenge you to...

Create Your Life (Chapter 1)

This chapter is all about discovering the real you, beneath the noise, the labels, and the pressure to fit in. Before confidence comes clarity: **knowing who you are and owning it.**

Use the prompts in this chapter to explore your values, uncover the parts of yourself you've hidden or ignored, and take your first steps toward real self-awareness. No rush. No pressure. Just honest reflection.

STEP INTO THE STORY

Think about Olivia's situation. Have you ever felt pressured to act in a way that didn't sit well with you? What did you do? How did it feel? What might you do differently now?

(Write as much or as little as you want – just don't cheat yourself!)

_____

_____

_____

_____

_____

_____

_____

_____

_____

_____

WHO ARE YOU REALLY?

What are some things you love about who you are? What are some things you value? (Dig down and give at least three!)

_____

_____

_____

_____

_____

_____

_____

_____

_____

BREAKING UP WITH LABELS

List any labels you've been given or that you've taken on. Then, next to each, write whether it feels true, and if it limits or empowers you.

_____

_____

_____

_____

_____

_____

_____

_____

_____

ESCAPE THE COMPARISON TRAP

Think about a time you compared yourself to someone else (online or in real life). What were you comparing? How did it make you feel? Was that comparison fair or helpful?

_____

_____

_____

_____

_____

_____

_____

_____

_____

WHAT MAKES YOU *YOU*?

Make a list of the things that make you unique—skills, quirks, passions, experiences, etc.

_____

_____

_____

_____

_____

_____

_____

_____

_____

_____

YOU ARE NOT ALONE

Do you know the feeling of being the last one picked for a team in gym class?

Yeah - that was how the entirety of middle school felt for me.

When homeschooling took my cousin away, the new reality hit hard.

At the start of seventh grade, it seemed like *everyone* had a group they belonged to – it was just a natural progression from elementary school. That didn't bode well for the new kid.

I would get on the bus every morning and put on headphones to drown out the teasing, but I could still feel the pounding on the back of my seat. I avoided eye contact in the hallways because that only led to more taunting - it felt like I was swimming with sharks. Many days, I didn't eat lunch because, let's face it - walking around with a tray of food and nowhere to go is just plain humiliating. What made it even worse was the culture shock - my new school was in the "country" (well, country enough for me), and I was from the "city." Not only could I not relate to these people, but I was an easy target for them.

I remember asking my mom to take me clothes shopping one day, telling her I wanted to throw everything away and start over. "I feel so stupid wearing this stuff!!" I would cry. It was just too hard, sticking out like a sore thumb. I *wanted* attention, but the fear of *negative* attention kept me in a defeating loop, and I didn't know how to break free. I didn't even know where to begin.

Yes, school was absolutely terrifying to me, and being home wasn't much better because *all I could think about was school*. No one understood what I was going through. My brother had a much easier time fitting into fourth grade - those kids weren't vicious yet. My *old* friends were doing fine, too - they were in the same town with the same friends. Over time, I didn't even talk to my best friend anymore. Life sadly took us our separate ways.

Every night, I dreaded falling asleep because I didn't want to face the next day. The harsh truth of this new reality quickly set in - I was utterly alone.

THE SAD REALITY OF FEELING ALONE

It is natural for teenagers to feel alone. Sad, but true. For centuries, young people have been going through the same struggles and feeling the same way. A simple question to your parents, aunts, or uncles will probably reveal stories similar to the one I just shared. Unfortunately, it's a part of life - but we must make amends with it to continue on the path to self-confidence.

Oddly enough, it's even common to feel like the friendships you DO have are superficial or shallow. You may find yourself desiring something more meaningful (this makes chapter one all the more critical - it's much harder to connect with people if you aren't sure about who you are). You want to be understood - we all do. And if you feel alone right now, recognizing those who have gone through it before can help soothe the pain. Ironically, knowing that others feel alone can help you feel *less* alone.

At the time of writing this, over half of Americans report feeling "alone." 73% of Gen Z'ers feel lonely sometimes or always. Social media may only worsen this, blurring the lines between real friends, acquaintances, and role models. 71% of heavy social media users say they often experience feelings of loneliness. In fact, one study found that the reduced use of social media *significantly* reduced loneliness and depression (Hartman 2022).

I'm not saying "get off social media," but instead making a point that it can complicate things for many people these days. And if your feelings of loneliness/depression are that bad, it would definitely be wise to keep social media in check. That said, there are other things you can do to alleviate the feeling of being alone.

1. **Join a club or team sport.** This is a great way to make friends who share your interests, and you can have fun together outside of school.
2. **Reach out to family and peers.** They are probably happy to listen (and might even be relieved that you finally talked to them about how you've been feeling). Parents may have gone through something similar and can offer advice or support. And

even if you don't feel like you have anything in common with someone, talking can still help.

3. **Get a pet.** This helped me a LOT (RIP, Sugan)! It is proven that pets can help with emotional support and the release of oxytocin (a chemical in the brain that promotes trust, empathy, and bonding). Who doesn't like a furry cuddle buddy?

4. **Be active and get outside.** Go for a run, walk, or bike ride. Spend time in nature. Exercise releases endorphins, which have mood-boosting effects. And being in nature has also been shown to improve mental well-being.

5. **Volunteer.** Helping others is a great way to feel needed and appreciated while providing support during tough times. You can meet lots of new people getting involved in the community. There are endless volunteer opportunities, including schools, food banks, hospitals, and animal shelters.

6. **Stay mindful.** Although loneliness may seem all-encompassing in the moment, remember that it is not permanent. Make sure to know the facts of your situation, and don't distort your thoughts to exaggerate how bad it is. Be present and take comfort in knowing that you are working on improving *every aspect* of your life right now.

BROKEN HOMES

Examples of broken homes are homes where one or both parents are absent, homes where the parents are divorced or separated, or homes where there is physical or emotional abuse.

Victims of Abuse

I will be honest - I don't feel equipped to give in-depth advice to serious abuse victims. Abuse is a heavy subject that requires urgent action and attention. However, after some research, I will say that you must not stay quiet in this case. As scary as it may be, keeping quiet will only further the abuse and hurt more people. Tell a family member, doctor, teacher, or any trusted adult - and if they don't respond appropriately, keep telling more adults until someone DOES. If this doesn't work, there are also many hotlines you can turn to by searching "Childhelp," "Child Helpline," or "Domestic/Violence Abuse Hotline." And, of course, if you need help immediately, call 911.

Split Families

Being a teenager is hard enough, but it can be especially difficult for those with divorced parents. Divorce often leaves children feeling lost and uncertain. You might feel like you're stuck in the middle and without the same stable home life that other families have. But it's crucial to remember that perspective is everything. Just because your family is different doesn't mean it's any less valid or important. Every family is special and unique in its own way.

You might even think that a broken home is your fault. That somehow, if you had just been better or tried harder, your family would still be together. But that is most certainly never true. Sometimes grownups can't get along, and that has nothing to do with you. It's usually the *opposite*. Parents will tend to try and "stay together for the kids," thinking they can hide their issues for the sake of their child's happiness. In this case, staying together can cause severe and deep resentment down the road. The unhappiness can also cause a toxic environment that children pick up on. It is much healthier for children and teens to see how to properly resolve issues rather than push them under the rug and become emotionally blocked (Schwartz 2021).

Sometimes, divorced families can be higher functioning than families who are still together! This was the case with my ex-wife (the mother of my children) and me. We got married young and tried to make it work for various reasons, including the well-being of our kids. It was clear that we didn't "work," and we decided to get a divorce. Since then, we have operated together amazingly - talking and coordinating daily and showing our kids that we are still family. Better yet, with their stepmom and stepdad, our kids now have *four* parents who love them and would do anything for them.

Everyone comes from different backgrounds and experiences, with a home life to match. What matters is how you deal with the hand you've been dealt. Are you loving and kind to your family? Do you communicate effectively? Do you take care of yourself and your responsibilities? That's what counts in the end. Learn to embrace your family, and just like with your personality, its differences.

OTHERS MAY JUST BE BETTER AT HIDING IT

 *"I prefer to surround myself with people who reveal their imperfection, rather than people who fake their perfection."*

— CHARLES F. GLASSMAN

Consider the story of Tom. Tom came across as the epitome of popularity on multiple social media platforms. He portrayed a pretty perfect teenage life by constantly showing off his family's cars, new clothes, and a cheesy smile. His comments section overflowed with sentiments like "You're so lucky!!" and "Must be nice to be you!!" Tom indeed built up some impressive follower counts for doing basically nothing - until he was eventually exposed as a fake. The cars were his cousin's, and the clothes were cheap rip-offs. He barely knew his dad, and his mother worked multiple jobs to support the two of them. It turned out he was trying to work towards getting paid advertising so he could help her out. It's actually very sad…

The point here is that things are rarely what they seem. Just because someone's life looks perfect doesn't mean that it *is*. People are good at hiding their struggles. And just because you don't see them it doesn't mean they don't exist. Remember this when thinking someone has it "so much better" than you. The grass isn't greener on the other side - it's greener where you water it.

And trust me, it's not just teenagers faking it - adults do it all the time! And it happens on both ends of the spectrum. Very successful people often have many personal problems - usually, the more successful someone is, the more pressure they feel to maintain that image. In this case, they might put on a happy face in front of friends or family to hide their struggles. And then you have people who are unhappy and perhaps unsuccessful. Like Tom, these people may portray a life that's better than it actually is to feel better about themselves – or to have their egos fed. Either example ends up being harmful in the long run for everyone.

For our purposes, the goal here is - yep, you guessed it! - becoming aware of it. Others are lonely too. Others do irrational things to hide the pain, too. Pretending to be someone you're not is potentially dangerous, but so is feeling jealous or less about yourself by comparison. These things directly oppose true self-confidence.

We've begun to lay the groundwork with some introspective principles. This foundation is necessary before making further substantial changes. But now it's time to get into some magical stuff - so hang on because the next chapter is one of my favorites! But first...

Create Your Life (Chapter 2)

This chapter explores a feeling many teens (and people in general) know too well: **loneliness.** Even when surrounded by others, it can feel like no one *really* understands. But here's the truth—you're not alone in feeling alone.

Use this chapter to reflect on your experiences, your relationships, and your home life. You'll also get to shift your perspective and challenge some of the assumptions you've been carrying.

WHAT DOES LONELINESS FEEL LIKE FOR YOU?

Write about a time you felt left out or disconnected. What helped (or what could have helped)?

_____

_____

_____

_____

_____

_____

_____

_____

_____

_____

REFLECT ON YOUR HOME LIFE.

Is it different from your friends'? What makes your family unique or challenging? List both struggles and strengths.

_____

_____

_____

_____

_____

_____

_____

_____

_____

▊ HOW DOES SOCIAL MEDIA AFFECT YOUR FEELINGS OF LONELINESS?

Be honest—do you compare your life to others' online? Does it lift you up or bring you down?

_____

_____

_____

_____

_____

_____

_____

_____

_____

•• THINK OF PEOPLE YOU KNOW (OR FOLLOW) WHO SEEM TO HAVE IT ALL TOGETHER.

Now imagine what they might be struggling with beneath the surface. It doesn't have to be accurate or true. This is just a brainstorming session to open your mind to the possibility that not everyone has it easy!

_____

_____

_____

_____

_____

_____

_____

_____

_____

_____

IF YOUR LONELINESS COULD SPEAK, WHAT WOULD IT SAY?

What does it *need* from you? Try to have a conversation with it here on the page.

_____

_____

_____

_____

_____

_____

_____

_____

_____

_____

3

THE POWER OF PERCEPTION (HOW YOUR THOUGHTS CREATE YOUR REALITY)

Trey woke up on a Saturday morning, looked out the window, and instantly his heart sank. It was utterly gray, a raging storm. After a week of school, Trey looked forward to spending his Saturdays outdoors, playing sports, and hanging out with friends. But now, all of that was literally down the drain.

He plopped himself back down on the bed and turned on the TV. "Well, this day is ruined," he texted the group thread. As he looked out the window, Trey felt himself getting more and more annoyed. He decided to head downstairs and kill the leftover pizza in the fridge. After quickly scarfing it down, feeling sorry for himself and bothered by how the day was going, he felt boredom creeping in. He had nothing to do and no one to hang out with. He retired again to the TV upstairs, wishing he could just go back to sleep and start over again on Sunday.

The hours passed, and Trey's mood only got worse. Strangely enough, his friends didn't seem to mind as much as he did. "Why are they just fine with this?! This sucks!! They must be doing something without me." This new train of thought made him even more upset. He started feeling angry and resentful toward his friends now. He didn't realize it at the time, but he was making himself the victim of this circumstance.

As you might guess, his day didn't get any better. By the time nightfall rolled around, Trey was in a foul mood and decided to go to bed early. He tossed and turned to sleep, muttering to himself and wishing Sunday would suit his needs a little better.

Down the street, on the same Saturday morning, Alex also woke up to thunder and rain pounding on her window. Like many others, she looked forward to Saturdays as a day to go outside and adventure with her friends, maybe ride bikes to the mall or the movies. "No fun in the sun today," she thought sadly.

The skies were dark and ominous, but Alex determined there must still be a way to have a great weekend. So she brainstormed while it stormed.

"I might as well get my chores out of the way," she decided. And while vacuuming and thinking of possible ideas for the day, she even went the extra mile and did *additional* cleaning. Alex smiled, knowing this would earn her a bigger allowance plus bonus points with the parents. Once finished, she texted her friends to see what they were up to.

"We're not doing anything…looks crappy out," was the consensus.

"I'm stuck here with my cousin anyways," said her friend Lily. "She's not very fun lol."

"Why don't you all just come here?" Alex texted.

"Bring your cousin, Lil. Can't be that bad. I have games and movies and stuff…at least we'll all be stuck inside together!"

They all replied positively, saying their parents would drop them off and, within half an hour, were at her door. What followed was a weekend they would talk about for years to come.

The group spent hours playing games, telling stories, and eating until they couldn't anymore. They recorded a hilarious video they *still* rewatch and laugh at (it turns out Lily's cousin was pretty cool, with a great YouTube channel). When the storm died down that night, they went outside and ran around in the puddles. They even made it to the mall before it closed (Alex was glad for that extra cash in her pocket!), and all the girls slept over and had an equally awesome Sunday.

It had been a long time since Alex had such a fantastic experience. She was so grateful that she had taken the time to view it differently and see the potential for fun. She got all her weekend chores done in one day, made extra money, met a new friend, and had an awesome sleepover - with a great story to tell!

THE POWER OF YOUR THOUGHTS

What's the difference between these two stories? It was the *same day* in both. Why was one so miserable and one so great? What **one** factor could completely change a person's entire reality or experience of a day?

I'm sure you guessed it, as it's the title of the chapter. The deciding factor was *perception*. It was *how* each person decided to view the day – specifically, the **thoughts** they chose (yes - your thoughts are a decision). Neither Trey nor Alex could do anything about changing the weather, yet their point of view radically transformed their experience. And what is life, after all? It's simply a series of experiences.

What do you see in the image above? Do you see a vase? Or do you see two faces? You can choose to see either. And either way, you're right. In fact, you're **always** right. In your life experience, this principle works the same way. No matter how you choose to see events, people, circumstances, or the weather - life will deliver proof of your viewpoint. Think of your life as a mirror - the reflection on the outside *always* matches the inside.

> *"Whether you think you can, or you think you can't -you're right."*

— HENRY FORD

"When you change the way you look at things, the things you look at change."

— MAX PLANCK/DR. WAYNE DYER

The wisest people in history knew this to be true. The tomb of ancient Egyptian philosopher Hermes was uncovered with wonder and excitement thousands of years ago because people believed it held the greatest secret of the ages. Inside, they found a tablet with the words "As within, so without; as above, so below." This means that what we think or believe on the *inside* is what will be expressed in our world on the *outside* (Murphy 2011, 24). Or, the outside world is a reflection of our inner world. What an incredible truth - a real-life secret you should impress upon yourself as early as possible! I didn't fully grasp this until my mid-twenties, but man, if I did…

So here we are with one of the most valuable tools for building our reality. What will you do with this knowledge? Well, the first thing you should do is *start monitoring your thoughts*. And I mean, watch them like a hawk. Notice when things are bothering, annoying, or agitating you. Use these as "triggers" to keep tabs on the self-talk inside your head. Is there a different way you can look at the situation? Is there a different perspective you can take, an alternate "story" you can tell yourself? The answer is YES - always. Again, awareness comes into powerful play here:

The more aware you are of what you're thinking, the easier it is to separate yourself from your thoughts. Instead of *identifying* with your mind, be the USER of your mind - it's the most powerful tool in the world.

Like the faces & vase optical illusion, anything in your life can be looked at in multiple ways. It's not always black and white - you can think about a situation positively, negatively, or in any manner in between (there is also *no* thought). Let me give you a few everyday examples. To drive a point home, I'll use very polarizing thinking:

- You wake up in the morning and brush your teeth. You could be thinking, "Ugh, I hate brushing my teeth. It's so annoying." You could just as well be thinking, "I'm grateful to have healthy teeth and gums and to be able to maintain them."
- A car accident causes standstill traffic, and you're stuck in it. You could think, "I'm going to be late! Why does this stuff always happen at the worst time?" – OR – "I'm lucky to be safe and sound, rather than in that accident."

- You're sitting in math class. "Math is SO boring; this class needs to be over!" – OR – "Maybe I'll try and learn something here today. Some kids don't even get the privilege of education."
- Dinner time, and it's lasagna - again. "I'm so sick of eating this, I just want a cheeseburger!" – OR – "Someone put a lot of time into making this. Come to think of it, some people would do anything for this meal."

The key to controlling your thoughts is **practice** and, more specifically - consistency. You don't master a sport in a day, and you don't learn an instrument overnight. Training your mind works the same way. Make the decision that you will become aware of your thoughts from now on. Decide to start choosing perspectives that empower you and **practice all the time**.

It might feel awkward or challenging when you first start "choosing" your thoughts - but the good news is that this gets easier. When we repeatedly think new thoughts, our brain cells begin to connect differently and create new patterns. These patterns, over time, will develop fresh "circuits" in our brains. This is called "neuroplasticity" (Dispenza 2019). Simply put, our new train of thought will become "normal" to us - it will slowly stop requiring as much effort.

I like to think of this process as having to do with a record player (hoping you know what those are!). The player's needle follows grooves in the record, and as it spins, it picks up vibrations that turn into sound. Think of your brain patterns as the grooves. If you leave the record playing, it will just continue along the same groove. But dig a new one and place the needle *there*, and now *that's* where it will continue to spin. Simple, right? We want to dig new, deeper grooves for our thoughts - then let the record spin.

DON'T TAKE IT PERSONALLY, BUT YOU'RE PROBABLY TAKING IT PERSONALLY

When it comes to the thoughts of others, there is often a large gap between what we *think* people are thinking of us and what they are *actually* thinking. How often have you felt self-conscious and said things to yourself like: "He probably thinks I look stupid…" or "She's definitely judging me." Or maybe "So-and-so has been quiet lately; they're avoiding me because they think I'm weird or annoying." I know I have. I was guilty of thinking that way for most of my teenage years. I *still* catch myself poorly imagining the thoughts of others from time to time.

Many people spend too much time and energy worrying about what others think of them. This is especially true during the teenage years when social status and acceptance are so important. The truth is that most of the time, we have no idea what other people think. Assuming negatively can lead to anger, resentment, and other harmful emotions.

In this case, we become our worst enemy, causing the needle to play along the pre-existing groove without even realizing it. Monitoring our thoughts becomes crucial, again, here. If **power** is contained in our thoughts, why would we give it away to others? Be patient and persistent with your efforts. Stay mindful and keep practicing your awareness.

Remember this: most of the time, nobody is concerned with you in the negative way you think! Even if they are, it's probably no more than a fleeting second. And half of the time, they're probably doing the *same thing* you are - worrying about what others think of *them*. Why not use your power to imagine people thinking GOOD things about you? If that sounds odd or weird, it's only because most of us aren't raised thinking this is even an option.

LIKE ATTRACTS LIKE

We've established that what you think about consistently, you bring about. This is one of the most fundamental laws of the universe, and it applies to everyone, regardless of age, race, or intelligence. But *why*? Looking at this phenomenon on a deeper level will give you a better understanding of the principle and help you apply it more confidently.

Call it whatever you'd like (and they do): Law of Attraction, Law of Vibration, Law of Assumption, manifestation, whatever - but don't get too wrapped up in words. When it comes to thoughts being energy - *like attracts like*. I don't know **how** it happens, but I know it **works**. I've practiced it for years and repeatedly received the proof in the pudding. Never mind that this is a masterful ancient concept or that almost *all* major religions teach it in one way or another (Singh 2020).

"If you want to find the secrets of the Universe, think in terms of energy, frequency and vibration."

— NIKOLA TESLA

"The mind attracts the thing it dwells upon."

— NAPOLEON HILL

"What you focus on expands, and when you focus on the goodness in your life, you create more of it."

— OPRAH WINFREY

In other words, our thoughts and beliefs tend to bring more of the "same" into our reality. Since we've already discussed how our thoughts create our reality, it's not a huge stretch to see how this would work.

If you think *negatively* about someone, you're going to be sending out *negative* vibes that will likely result in them treating you poorly. But if you think *positively* about someone, you're going to send out *positive* vibes that will likely result in them treating you well.

When thinking of yourself - if you believe that you are stupid or not good enough, you will likely experience circumstances that reflect those beliefs back to you. If you see yourself as valuable and worthy, on the other hand, others will too. People around you will treat you by how you think of *yourself*.

It sounds simple enough, but it's not always easy. Our minds are mighty, yet they often tend to dwell on negative things. That's why it's essential to be vigilant in watching your thoughts.

Think about it this way: *your current situation is the product of your previous ways of thinking.* From now on, try to get in the habit of thinking of yourself as a powerful, living, breathing magnet. You can use this mindset to create a success loop/pattern for every aspect of your life:

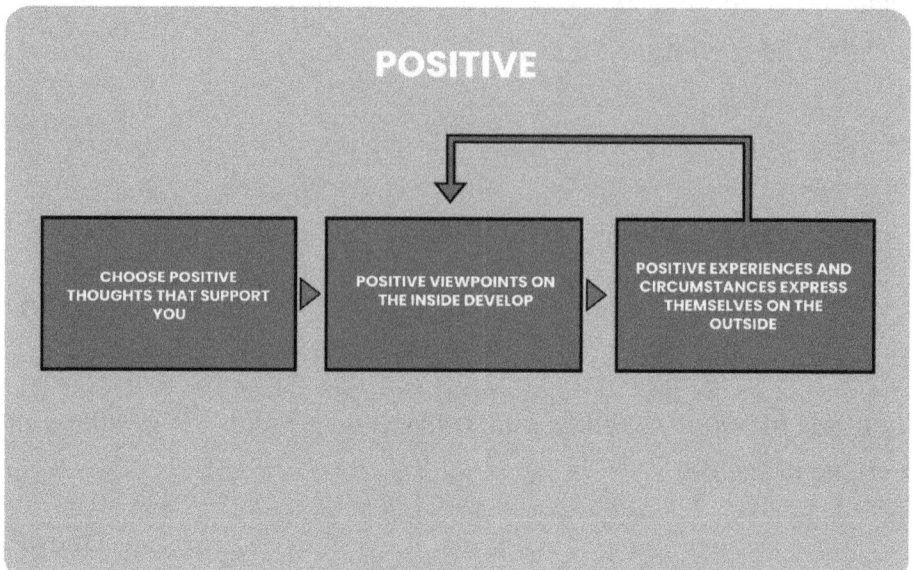

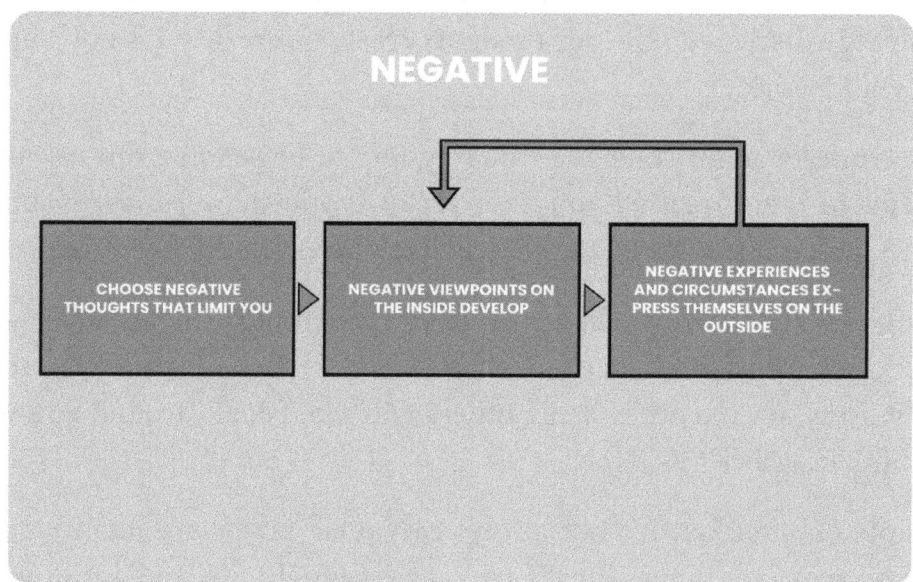

As shown above, once a thought pattern is started (often the most challenging part), it continues as a "loop," continuously feeding itself. Whether inputting positive thoughts, negative thoughts, or anything in between - it works the same way. Why do you think they say, "The rich get richer, and the poor get poorer"? Because, to a degree, it's true! Poor people are in the habit of *thinking* they're poor, while rich people are in the business of *thinking* rich. You are either adding to your life or taking away from it. So why wouldn't we choose to add amazing things to our input?

More often than not, people practically *live* in the negative loop. And this is not even because they choose to, necessarily. It's because 1) they aren't aware of their thought patterns, and 2) they're observing the outer "reality" they've created (based on previous thoughts) and continue to react to that reality. And it goes on, and on, and on. See how this could keep someone in a destructive cycle of creating what they don't want?

It's important to mention that once a positive pattern is in motion, it doesn't mean we stop "inputting" the things we desire. Or that it just runs on autopilot. We've made the process easier by digging the new groove, which over time, becomes more effortless and feels more natural. But keep feeding that machine new, better inputs! Soon, you will **want** to. Let's take it to the next level and learn how to do this *effectively*.

BUILDING NEW BELIEFS

Have a headache yet? It's a lot to think about if you've never considered the science of thought before, but utilize this chapter correctly, and it could easily be the most life-changing one in the book. And it wouldn't be complete without discussing **beliefs**.

We will not be discussing religious, moral, or ethical beliefs here. The dictionary describes belief as "an acceptance that a statement is true or that something exists." For our purposes, when I say belief, I mean: *a continued or repeated thought that becomes an inner truth to you*. Since beliefs are essentially looped thoughts, you'll find that they can be either limiting (restricting you) or empowering (supporting you).

Some examples of **limiting** beliefs may be:

- I'm not good enough
- I'm not very smart
- I am unlovable
- I must avoid failure
- People think I'm annoying
- It's impossible
- That's just the way things are
- Things will never change
- Life is hard
- Change is hard

Some examples of **empowering** beliefs:

- I am in control of my life
- I can do anything I put my mind to
- I am worthy of love and respect
- I am unique and special
- I deserve to be happy and successful
- I can handle whatever comes my way
- Everything happens for a reason
- I am open to new experiences and learning opportunities
- I am capable/competent
- Change is natural

Just like your power of perception as a whole, no beliefs are right or wrong. They are simply beliefs. And since they are made of thoughts, we can choose to change them, just like thoughts. Change your beliefs, and you will change your world.

 *"The outer conditions of a person's life will always be found to reflect their inner beliefs."*

— JAMES ALLEN

Because here's the thing: beliefs are *insanely* powerful. **Every single experience you have in life is filtered through your beliefs.** Your interpretation of events, people, and situations is based on the *totality* of your beliefs.

And it's not just major life events like getting a job or being in a relationship. Your beliefs also dictate how you feel about minor things, like whether you think you can parallel park or not.

You may already believe that you are a confident person. But if you believe that parallel parking is hard, then every time you do it, that belief will be reinforced - and you will likely struggle with it. On the other hand, if you believe that parallel parking is easy, then it likely will be. When our beliefs become "natural" to our way of thinking, when they embed themselves into our subconscious mind - they become empowered. So how do we empower our new beliefs?

REPETITION, REPETITION, REPETITION, REPETITION...

Beliefs can be enforced by visualizing, speaking, or thinking. But one constant must remain: repetition! New beliefs must be repeated over and over again until they become a part of your subconscious mind. And once they are there, they will start to shape your reality without you even having to think about it.

Repetition can be applied in many ways, including positive affirmations, vision boards or journals, and meditation.

Some people like to write their affirmations on index cards or post-it notes and carry them around to read throughout the day. Others prefer to record themselves saying their affirmations and listen to them regularly. The key is to find a method (or combination of methods) that works best for you and that you will DO!

I've done this for so long that I've gotten good at mentally repeating my desired beliefs and outcomes, *feeling* them true before they were physically tangible. But at the start, I used a combination of affirmations, vision boards, and journals. Anything which would help my subconscious mind **believe** what I was suggesting.

For example, one of my current empowering beliefs is "Everything is constantly working for me and for the greatest good." Whenever challenging moments arise, I feel this belief so deeply embedded in me that I instinctively rely on it - and it almost *always* presents itself to be "true" quite quickly. You are welcome to use that belief, but I encourage you to dig deep and find your own. Look at some of your fears, weaknesses, or doubts. How can you flip those around to make empowering beliefs out of them?

This may seem like a lot of work, but remember – *you want your beliefs working for you!* The more you can reinforce them, the more quickly they will become part of your subconscious mind and the faster they will start to shape your reality.

One final note: it is crucial to be aware of your **current** beliefs and any belief system you may have inherited from your family or society. Often, these belief systems are based on fear, scarcity, or lack - and can hold you back in life without you even realizing it. By becoming aware of these beliefs, you can start to question them and ultimately choose to change them if you desire.

"Whatever the mind can conceive and believe, it can achieve."

— W. CLEMENT STONE

"Therefore I tell you, whatever you ask for in prayer, believe that you have received it, and it will be yours."

— MARK 11:24

Create Your Life (Chapter 3)

This chapter is a turning point. Here's where you learn one of the most important truths of all: *Your thoughts shape your world.* The way you think about your life, your challenges, and even yourself—creates your experience of reality.

Use this workbook section to observe your thoughts, reflect on your beliefs, and start building new mental patterns that support the confident life you want.

🌀 REFLECT ON A RECENT SITUATION THAT FRUSTRATED YOU.

Let's focus on just one for now. What caused you frustration? Write that down, along with any thoughts that might have shaped your experience. Could a different perspective have changed it? Write down at least one different perspective you could've chosen.

_____

_____

_____

_____

_____

_____

_____

_____

_____

_____

START A THOUGHT AUDIT.

What are some recurring thoughts you have about school, friends, your body, or your abilities? Do they help or hurt you?

_____

_____

_____

_____

_____

_____

_____

_____

_____

_____

◎ WRITE DOWN FIVE FEARS, DOUBTS, OR NEGATIVE BELIEFS YOU'VE HAD.

Then, flip each into a new empowering belief. (Example: "I'm horrible at physical activity" could be flipped to "I'm getting slightly better in gym every week.") Practice thinking these new beliefs daily.

_____

_____

_____

_____

_____

_____

_____

_____

_____

_____

IMAGINE YOU ARE A MAGNET ATTRACTING MORE OF WHAT YOU THINK.

What have your thoughts been attracting lately? What would you like to start attracting instead? Focus only on what you *want* here, and list as many magnetizing thoughts as you can.

_____

_____

_____

_____

_____

_____

_____

_____

_____

_____

✳ WHAT'S ONE LIMITING BELIEF YOU WANT TO REWRITE?

Describe it, then rewrite it as a mantra or affirmation. Repeat it to yourself with confidence.

_____

_____

_____

_____

_____

_____

_____

_____

_____

_____

4

THE OLD MINDSET

I sincerely hope you are enjoying the journey so far. I hope you've been able to pick up on some new concepts or at least strengthen pre-existing ones. Most importantly, I hope you've begun to learn a little more about yourself. You may have never thought about where your self-esteem lies before. You may have never known about the power of your thoughts and how they affect your confidence levels, let alone your whole world.

The discovery of new concepts can be very stimulating. And the discovery of *yourself* will show you just how vast you are and that new things are always possible. The cool thing is that these discoveries continue throughout life. Exciting as that is, we still have a ways to go.

You can only absorb so much information at a time. It would be nice to use this chapter as an "intermission" point to step back and revalue current habits, traits, and potentially harmful ways of thinking. So take a breather from the reading, have some fun with the next section, and be completely honest with yourself so we can accurately move on to taking *action!*

CHECK-IN POINT

If it helps, you can consider this chapter a "survey." Go through each category and mark every box which applies to you. The end results will help you understand yourself more and let you know which direction to focus your attention on while moving forward.

IDENTITY

- ☐ I know my passions and what lights me up inside
- ☐ I am authentic and true to myself
- ☐ I have a strong sense of self-identity
- ☐ I know my strengths and weaknesses
- ☐ I have an accurate view of myself
- ☐ I accept myself for who I am
- ☐ My thoughts, feelings, and actions are in alignment
- ☐ I take responsibility for my life
- ☐ It is okay for me to be different from others
- ☐ I live by my values

WHAT STOOD OUT THE MOST TO YOU IN THIS SECTION?

HAPPINESS

- ☐ I smile and laugh often
- ☐ I enjoy time with friends and family
- ☐ I make time for myself, without feeling guilty about it
- ☐ I feel content living in the moment
- ☐ I embrace change
- ☐ It makes me feel good to do kind things for others
- ☐ I can be happy, even when things aren't going my way
- ☐ I have a sense of humor and can laugh at myself
- ☐ I can see the best in people and situations
- ☐ I don't need instant gratification and can resist temptation

WHAT STOOD OUT THE MOST TO YOU IN THIS SECTION?

HABITS

- □ I get enough sleep
- □ I am good about eating healthy foods
- □ I'm regularly active
- □ I spend time outdoors in nature
- □ I take breaks throughout the day to relax and rejuvenate
- □ I'm able to take risks and challenge myself
- □ I surround myself with positive people who support my well-being
- □ I know how to resolve conflicts peacefully
- □ I have good communication skills - both verbal and nonverbal
- □ I know how to set goals and work toward them

WHAT STOOD OUT THE MOST TO YOU IN THIS SECTION?

SELF-ESTEEM

- ☐ I like myself the way I am
- ☐ I feel good about myself most of the time
- ☐ If someone doesn't like me, that's their problem, not mine
- ☐ My thoughts and feelings are important and matter
- ☐ I deserve respect and appreciation from others, as well as myself
- ☐ I am a unique person with special talents and qualities
- ☐ Outer circumstances can't change the way I feel about myself
- ☐ I accept compliments gracefully
- ☐ I forgive myself for past mistakes
- ☐ I am focused on my strengths

WHAT STOOD OUT THE MOST TO YOU IN THIS SECTION?

MINDFULNESS

- ☐ I am generally aware of the thoughts I'm thinking
- ☐ My thoughts are serving me well
- ☐ My thoughts generate more positive than negative emotions
- ☐ I have control over my thoughts
- ☐ I am aware of the people in my life who might contribute to negative thought patterns
- ☐ I don't develop false beliefs about myself just because of negative thought patterns
- ☐ I don't allow the replaying of past events in my mind to affect the quality of my thinking process
- ☐ Stressful situations don't have control over my thoughts
- ☐ I allow any negative thoughts to be "fleeting," and I don't give them power
- ☐ I feel empowered thinking positive thoughts

WHAT STOOD OUT THE MOST TO YOU IN THIS SECTION?

❖ MINDSET SUMMARY

Add up the number of boxes you checked *for each category:*

7–10 = High: You're doing great here—keep it up!

4–6 = Moderate: There's room to grow—focus on a few small changes.

0–3 = Low: This area needs your attention. Be kind to yourself and use this workbook to grow.

🔍 WRITE YOUR SCORE FOR EACH CATEGORY AND REFLECT ON WHAT YOU'D LIKE TO WORK ON:

MY MINDSET MAP

Now that you've seen your mindset snapshot, let's set your direction:

- One area I want to grow in most:

_____

- A mindset I want to let go of:

_____

- A belief or habit I want to build:

_____

- One action I'll take this week to move forward:

_____

Remember—awareness is the first step toward change.

INTERNAL WORK > EXTERNAL FORCES

It's important to continuously look at our current habits and ways of thinking and see if they're serving us or not. This means being truthful with ourselves and shining a light on the parts of our mindsets that no longer help us. This practice can protect us from any destructive external forces that come our way.

As a teenager, you may experience "external forces" in the form of:

- peer pressure
- social media
- academic stress
- parental expectations
- body image standards
- competitiveness with others
- the need to belong
- fear of failure

Don't get overwhelmed - once you've done the groundwork of rooting your self-esteem, no external force can shake it. You'll start finding yourself immune to the opinions of others; you'll no longer need their approval to feel good about yourself. Your self-worth will come from within, invincible and untouchable by anyone or anything.

"It is not the beauty of a building you should look at; it's the construction of the foundation that will stand the test of time."

— DAVID ALLAN COE

A strong house foundation is essential for a safe and sturdy home. It's the same with self-confidence: a stable mindset is key to feeling good about yourself and thriving, especially during these developmental years. Just like a strong foundation can withstand any storm, a person with a stable mindset can weather any challenge. But none of us are perfect - not even close. So I'm sure you wouldn't mind a couple of life hacks to keep you on track...

PATTERN INTERRUPTS

A pattern interrupt is any action that breaks the cycle of unwanted thinking. It can be as simple as taking a deep breath, changing the subject, or snapping a rubber band on your wrist (it sounds weird, but it works). The important thing is that it interrupts the flow of negative thoughts and allows you to start fresh.

Remember when we talked about "neuroplasticity" in the brain, the ability to develop new circuits which create thought patterns? Well, a proper interrupt can be very effective at immediately **stopping** the harmful patterns.

But anyways, what are you having for dinner tonight? I'm probably going to have some chicken, fries, and veggies. Although what I really want is lobster. Or sushi...I haven't had sushi in so long!

No, I haven't lost my mind - that was a pattern interrupt! You were reading along, and your brain got comfortable, running on autopilot, when BAM! - something unexpected came and pulled you out of it, redirecting your focus. This is how you want to deal with unwanted thoughts. As soon as you become aware of a thought you know isn't good for you, hit it with a pattern interrupt.

Yes, you can make a pattern interrupt out of *anything* that instantly breaks up your thinking - but here are a few more ideas:

- sing your favorite song out loud
- repeat a positive affirmation five times
- put on some music
- do five jumping jacks or push-ups
- splash water on your face
- pick an exciting word to shout

If you have problems with negative thoughts running wild, pick a pattern interrupt that works best for you and start putting it into place!

And now all I'm thinking about is sushi.

FAKE IT TILL YOU MAKE IT (SORT OF)

This common saying could be taken negatively. You might ask, "Why would I want to pretend to be something I'm not? Doesn't that go *against* 'finding yourself'?" And you would be right. So instead, think of this phrase as becoming the person you *choose* to be rather than the person you think you're *supposed* to be. Let me also be clear that I'm talking about *projecting good qualities* - not about lying or putting yourself in serious situations if you are not competent.

You're not "faking it" for the sake of someone else. In fact, "fake it till you make it" isn't even really correct (but hey, it rhymes and is easy to remember). In reality, you're "practicing it until you perfect it" (Clark 2016). You're in line with your true self, at a level of awareness where you **know** the person you want to be. And even though you're not quite "there" yet, you'll practice living that way.

You might not believe it, but people will treat you differently when they think you're confident. In turn, this will make *you* feel more confident. It's a self-fulfilling prophecy.

How do you see yourself? Want to be funnier? Start making jokes, even if they're corny. Want to be more outgoing? Join clubs and organizations, volunteer, attend social events, and meet new people. Want to practice confidence before you truly feel it? Stand up straight, make eye contact, and speak slowly and clearly. Dress the part - wear clothes that make you feel good about yourself. You don't need designer labels, just something that makes you feel put together and presentable. As long as you are consistent with your true self, this will propel you to your target.

The point of this little trick is to **practice new behaviors until they become second nature.** It's the "action" version of practicing your thoughts until they dig new grooves. It may feel strange at first - you may not believe the person you're pretending to be is really you. But, like so many other techniques in this book - it works. The more you act like the person you want to be, the easier it becomes to believe that's who you are.

One more thing. It's imperative to mention that you must go at your own pace. You should never feel too far out of line, to the point where you DO feel "fake." Don't force anything! If you feel like that's the case, reevaluate your intentions, slow down, and get back to feeling like YOU.

5

WHAT DRIVES YOU?

It was the start of eighth grade. After a year of shielding myself emotionally (and physically), not much changed. My skin was a little thicker, and my style was slightly more "amended" to fit in with the new environment. I didn't hate school as much, but I certainly wouldn't say I liked it. I still didn't have real friends. And I most definitely wasn't expressing myself.

Little did I know, while sluggishly meandering to class one day, that everything was about to change - big time.

I remember the moment clearly. It was Spanish class right before lunch. I walked in about five minutes early to find only a handful of kids in the room - two talking at their desks, one in the front row studying, and then, way in the back - Rory.

Rory was a rare middle school exception. Everyone knew him, and everyone loved him - but he was a loner. He was tall, full-framed, and *reeked* of confidence. I never did understand it. It was annoying.

Anyways. On this day, in the very back of the class, I noticed a guitar case strapped to Rory's back (he was one of the only kids who could pull this off). Now sitting at my desk, I found my eyes glued to him. He was kind of mesmerizing, like a teenage unicorn. He pulled out a blue Fender Strat, threw the case on the floor, and sat with the guitar on his knee.

I watched the desk buckle a bit as he shifted his weight, and then, as if no one else in the room existed, he started playing. Although it was quiet, my ears perked up. "I know this song!" I thought. Now, I'm going to date myself here - but the song was "Undone (The Sweater Song)" by Weezer. Not only did I know the song, but it was part of the album I currently blasted on the bus to drown out the world. To date myself again - I played that *CD* until it physically didn't work anymore.

"Ok…so what?" you might say. Well, I still can't quite explain the feeling that occurred at that moment, but I'll try. Every hair on my body stood on edge. It was a feeling I had never experienced before, one that I can only describe as "awe." Kind of like every single cell in my body was shouting at me simultaneously, "You need to learn more about this!!" Someone was replicating a piece of music I loved *so* effortlessly and gracefully. If he could do that, why couldn't I? What was *stopping* me?

I determined the answers to those questions by the end of the day. I *could* do that. And *nothing* was stopping me.

And that's all it took. I remembered hearing from my parents that my uncle owned a little music shop in the neighboring state. I told my mom that night that I wanted him to set me up with a guitar. I made it very clear to her that it was *all* I wanted. My mom, being a very cool rock mom, didn't hesitate. And a few weeks later, right around my 14th birthday, I was presented with a Stratocaster of my own.

It wasn't a Fender Strat; it was a cheap knock-off. But that didn't matter. The sense of purpose that thing gave me was insane. And it felt so right. I played every single day, chopping down the basics piece by piece and then getting more technical. Anything I wanted to learn, I just **did it** - I did it until the sloppiness turned into perfection. After about a year of playing, my mother took me in for lessons. Well, five or six classes deep, the instructor told me, "There's not really much more that I can teach you…". I now know this wasn't true. But true or not, it empowered me even *more*. So I continued teaching myself, getting even better.

A cool side effect I found along the way was that other "issues" in my life seemed to disappear magically. They just took care of themselves. My mind was no longer getting in my way. It was the total opposite - I was focused and loving it. I was attracting totally new experiences which matched my passion, and people started treating me differently. I'm not saying everything was rainbows and butterflies after this or that the credits rolled, and it was my perfect happy ending. But there *was* a significant shift on many levels.

As I mentioned in the introduction, this was the beginning of a massive part of my life. I begged my brother and cousin to learn drums and bass, and I made sure they practiced just as much as I did! Fast forward a couple of years, and the biggest local radio station ended up playing one of our songs. It became so popular that they invited us to be a part of their annual festival show, to play in front of over 25,000 people. That was our third show ever. And we were all still teenagers.

Maybe in another book, I'll go into the incredible decade that followed. But for our purposes here, this is the point I want to get across:

I had no idea that this one little moment - this seemingly tiny blip of inspiration on my timeline - could become the driving force of my life. I found myself by following my passion. Countless doors were opened. I truthfully no longer cared what others thought of me. I felt invincible. I became the **definition** of self-confidence.

FIND YOUR PASSION(S)

 *"Light yourself on fire with passion and people will come from miles to watch you burn."*

— JOHN WESLEY

I am not telling you to start a band or necessarily even suggesting it. What I *am* telling you to do is find *your* passion. This is when you shift from the interior to the exterior - when you begin expressing yourself. You have worked to discover who you are, and now it is time to start showing what makes you special - allowing your one-of-a-kind personality to shine, radiating the world with your true colors.

Let's dig in. Remember this: passion is anything that lights you up inside. It's the object of your love. And it doesn't have to be limited to one thing - some people pursue many passions. There's no right or wrong when it comes to what you love. You may already have a good idea of what you're passionate about, and that's great! But what if you have **no clue**? How *do* you find your passion?

1. **Ask yourself what you enjoy doing most.** What activities make you lose track of time? That is a great question to ask yourself. I know that when I'm immersed in something I love, the hours fly by. It doesn't matter how small or insignificant it may seem. You don't have to change the world (yet). Do you love playing video

games? Reading? Writing? Is there a specific type of music you get lost in? A sport? Maybe cooking is your thing? Although music is still a great passion of mine, more recently, I've discovered that I get lost in my writing. That's a clear sign to me. Recall your past days, weeks, and months - what things are genuinely delightful to you? Make a list of as many as you can.

2. **Look for activities that come *naturally* to you.** Everyone has certain activities or skills that come more easily than others. What are yours? These things might be slightly different than what you *enjoy* doing most. Do you have any talents/abilities/quirks? Perhaps people often tell you that you're "a natural" at something that you might typically brush off as "normal." Maybe it's not even that *fun* to you, but you're **good** at it. Make a list of these things, too.

3. **Don't be afraid to try new things!** Exploration is a vital part of finding out what you love. You may never know what you're passionate about if you don't venture outside your comfort zone. If you're not the type who typically tries new things, this may be a challenge for you - but it could be well worth it in the end. Again referring to my own experience, I never in a million years would have considered playing guitar before that moment. It never even crossed my mind. Maybe that's why it was so invigorating. There are SO many things in life to experience. It could be an excellent thing for you to discover something new. Think outside the box and write down a few activities, sports, or hobbies that might *intrigue* you.

4. **Pay attention to your feelings.** Throughout life, your emotions are going to be your ultimate guide. You'll know you're on the right track to finding your passion when you feel good inside - when something aligns with the person you want to be and your authenticity. When you feel like something just "clicks." You may get goosebumps, butterflies, or even tears. You will know. And once you do, it's an incredible feeling. Now write down a list of the *qualities* of your life that make you feel good. These could be simple sentiments, from "I feel great when I'm with a group of like-minded people" to "I cherish animals." We'll get back to these lists at the end of the chapter.

CELEBRATING UNIQUENESS

Often in discovering what drives them, teenagers may feel embarrassed or afraid to embrace the things that potentially make them "different." Please make no mistake - your uniqueness is pure power.

How does that phrase go? Oh yeah - "follow the leader." You know why? Because no one *follows the follower*. Don't strive to be a cookie-cutter mold of someone else! It took me far too long to grasp this - the sooner **you** do, the better.

Bruce Lee. Barack Obama. Lady Gaga. Prince. Muhammad Ali. Taylor Swift. Tiger Woods. Ellen DeGeneres. The list goes on and on. What comes to mind when you think of these inspirational people? If you said "individuality," "leadership," or "distinctiveness," you would be correct on all counts. You may be a little quirky. You might have an unusual style. Start to view this as a **great** thing as you dive into your passion. We scratched the surface of this in "Escaping the Comparative Trap" in chapter one, but now it's time to bring it to life and *express* it.

More often than not, most don't realize until adulthood (if ever) that our quirks are indeed our superpowers - our imprint on the world, our ability to become the leader instead of the follower. The paradox is that this way of thinking may completely oppose the pressure you feel to conform. But the truth is that people (especially young people) want to be inspired by others - we *look* to others for inspiration.

Did you know that Taylor Swift was teased and ignored because she used to stay home and write songs instead of going to parties with her friends?

Think about the ground-breaking achievements of Barack Obama, and imagine a world without him!

Let the examples of the greats be an encouragement. Learn to break the mold. Be YOU - that's your advantage. And most certainly, do not let the fear of what others think stop you from pursuing your passion.

A SENSE OF PURPOSE FEELS AMAZING

When honing in on and nurturing your passions, you will naturally develop something you may have never felt before - a sense of purpose.

And what a satisfying feeling that is. You'll feel more alive, noticing a newfound depth to life. You'll feel more in control of yourself and your happiness. Your sense of purpose will begin to work hand in hand with your identity development. Research shows that young adults feel more profound satisfaction, joy, and even better health when seeking purpose in their lives (Cook-Deegan 2015).

A few years back, I read "The Alchemist" by Paulo Coelho. It is a fantastic story (fable, really) about a shepherd boy named Santiago who goes on a journey to find his "Personal Legend." If you haven't read it, I highly recommend doing so. Basically, your Personal Legend is what you are meant to do in life - your purpose. In the book, Santiago realizes that he receives messages from the "Soul of the World" when he dreams. The Soul of the World is telling him what his Personal Legend is and nudging him to take steps towards achieving it. At first, he doesn't believe it. But as time goes on, he realizes that everything in his life has led him to this one thing. And once he accepts it and begins following his heart, everything falls into place, and miraculous things start happening.

That may sound a bit woo-woo, but I resonated with this book. It made me realize that we all have a "personal legend" or a destiny - and it is our job to follow it. When you find your personal legend and begin pursuing it, you will start to feel more fulfilled than you ever have before. You will be surprised at how effortless things become because you'll finally live in alignment with who you are meant to be.

Your sense of purpose must **never** be defined by someone else. It's one of the most personal things you can discover. Allowing others to limit or alter your purpose will lead to an unfulfilled life, settlement, and maybe even worse things, such as extreme depression and detachment.

Let your newfound sense of purpose become the North Star by which you are guided. It will be a source of strength and motivation on tough days - a reminder of why you're doing what you're doing when you feel like giving up. Even the most mundane tasks will begin to feel more worthwhile. You will start to see your life as a series of building blocks, each taking you closer to the best version of yourself.

 *"He who has a why to live can bear almost any how."*

— FRIEDRICH NIETZSCHE

You'll find that this chapter also parallels chapter three, which is intentional. We can now use the "like attracts like" principle in full force.

Feeling good and being happy are like muscles that are strengthened when exercised. As you dig into your passions, magnetism and momentum will bring you more things to feel good about. Set aside time for this! Don't be surprised if amazing people and circumstances start coming into your life simply because of doing what you love.

I'm excited for you to discover what drives you and, ultimately, your sense of purpose. Just don't forget about me when you're big-time, ok?

Create Your Life (Chapter 5)

This is a special chapter—because it's about unlocking what fuels your confidence from the inside out. Discovering your passion isn't just exciting, it's deeply transformative. Let's explore what lights you up and how it can become your compass. (*Note: it's ok if there are repeating answers in the coming prompts.*)

WHAT ACTIVITIES MAKE YOU LOSE TRACK OF TIME?

List things you love doing, no matter how small.

_____

_____

_____

_____

_____

_____

_____

_____

_____

_____

WHAT COMES NATURALLY TO YOU?

What skills or traits do others point out in you (even if you overlook them)?

_____

_____

_____

_____

_____

_____

_____

_____

_____

_____

🔍 WHAT NEW THINGS HAVE YOU ALWAYS BEEN CURIOUS ABOUT?

List activities or hobbies that intrigue you—even if you've never tried them.

_____

_____

_____

_____

_____

_____

_____

_____

_____

🩶 WHAT QUALITIES MAKE YOU FEEL THE MOST ALIVE OR ALIGNED WITH WHO YOU REALLY ARE?

This is one specific to *qualities*, as opposed to hobbies or activities you enjoy. (Again, although these prompts might seem similar, they are specifically different for a reason!)

_____

_____

_____

_____

_____

_____

_____

_____

_____

_____

YOUR PASSION PATTERN

Look back at your lists. What shows up more than once? Are there overlaps between things you love, are good at, and are curious about?

List your top 3 themes or passions here:

1. _____

2. _____

3. _____

CREATE YOUR PASSION POSTER

Use this page to sketch or describe your dream version of YOU doing what you love. Include things like where you are, what you're doing, how you feel, and who you're inspiring.

Not an artist? No problem. Use words, shapes, arrows, lists—just make it yours.

6

THE FIRST "B" WORD

The next two chapters are sore spots for me. I almost didn't want to include them because they still make me feel squeamish and uneasy. But then I realized that's precisely why I *had* to include them - they're touchy but necessary subjects that will directly impact your confidence levels. This is as much a catharsis for me as it may be for you!

Body image is something that SO many people struggle with - not just teens. Unfortunately, developing a negative body image when you are younger can set you up for a life of self-loathing if not dealt with properly. Other unfortunate downsides for teens: you're going through many physical changes right now, and you have way too many others around to compare yourself to.

As I was researching and going through statistics, I found myself getting sad. It is very important to me to 1) do my best in fleshing out this topic and 2) provide some insight and relief. When I was your age, I was extremely self-conscious about my looks. I was constantly comparing myself to others and convinced everyone was watching and judging me. I thought that people would like me more if I just lost a few pounds, changed my hair, or got my skin to clear up. I was ultimately wrong. But then again, I hadn't yet begun the foundational journey you're embarking on now.

Data such as facts and statistics can help you become more aware, change your thinking patterns, and begin to overcome a negative body image.

Regarding teen body image and self-esteem

- As many as 61% of adolescents are not content with their physical appearance.
- 53% of all American girls aged thirteen are unhappy with their bodies.
- 28% of 15-year-old girls are on diets.
- 14% of boys are dissatisfied with their weight or their figures.
- 94% of teen girls and 64% of teen boys have experienced body shaming.

(Soocial 2022)

- In a study of various teenagers, self-esteem "consistently hinges" on how attractive they see themselves.
- Compared to teenage boys, teen girls are likelier to be unhappy with their bodies and have lower self-esteem.
- 80% of 17-year-old girls are uncomfortable with their physical appearance and worry about becoming overweight.
- 17% of adolescent boys who are an average weight think they are too skinny.
- Underweight adolescent boys are more likely to be dissatisfied with their bodies and have lower self-esteem.

(Salt Effect 2022)

WHAT IS BODY IMAGE?

Body image is a person's mental representation of their physical appearance. It includes both the way that person sees themself and how they think other people see them. A positive body image is vital for building self-confidence because it means a person is comfortable and confident in their own skin. They are not constantly worrying about how they look or comparing themselves to others.

My teen years were in the '90s. School, for me, was the most significant source of impact on my body image, along with TV and the start of social media (AOL and MySpace!). I can only imagine growing up now with social media as normal as breathing. In fact, I can see the effects of it on my pre-teen children. With perfect filters and edited photos, it's hard not to feel like you're constantly being compared to others. This comparison can lead to (consciously or subconsciously) lower self-esteem and tons of body image issues, which can ruin your confidence before you even start to develop it.

Awareness (there's that word again) alone of social media's influence on you can start to disempower it. But there are other culprits out there to be mindful of as well:

1. **Family**. Your parents and siblings will naturally have a significant influence on you, as you spend most of your life with them! A parent's concern about their weight is often impressed onto their children, whether they intend it or not, simply by telling *their* story.
2. **Peers**. We will talk all about peers in chapter eight. For now, understand this: spending time with friends or acquaintances who are obsessed with weight and appearance and who frequently discuss others' bodies or their own negatively has the potential to harm **your** body image. Fortunately, the opposite is also true.
3. **Celebrities**. This is a big one and pretty self-explanatory. Seeing images of so-called "perfect" beauty leads to more unhappiness with one's own body, increased depression, and lower self-esteem. A study shows that 80% of teenage girls compare themselves to images of celebrities, and half said that these celebrity images make them feel dissatisfied with the way they look (Newport Academy 2018). Just because body image issues are more common among teenage girls than boys doesn't mean that *anyone* can't be affected by them.
4. **YOU**. Your mental health will directly affect your body image - another reason why it's so crucial to focus on the inside work first. Also, past negative experiences can subconsciously haunt you for quite a long time if not dealt with properly.

In this chapter, I hope to give some solid advice and suggestions regarding a negative body image. If you're one of the luckier ones who are already happy in this department, don't stop reading. Sometimes it can be very beneficial to see things from other people's perspectives!

Start by asking yourself:

- How do I feel when I look in the mirror?
- Do I compare my body to others often?
- What are things that make me feel good about my body?
- Do I have any physical features that I dislike or wish were different?
- When was the last time I felt pleased with how my body looked?
- Do negative thoughts about my body impact other areas of life?

DEALING WITH CHANGE

When "teenagers," "body image," and "change" all join the mix, it brings to mind the elephant in the room - puberty. Growth spurts, acne, voice changes, mood swings, emotional ups and downs, and...hair. Well, guess what? That's it for the discussion on puberty.

I don't think you need *me* to tell you about these things. There are plenty of other, better sources for that, such as parents and teachers. Instead, I'd like to take a bigger look at "change." Once we understand *what change is*, we can easily apply it to our ever-changing bodies.

 *"Change is the only constant in life."*

— HERACLITUS, GREEK PHILOSOPHER

Did you know that your cells are dying and regenerating all the time? You're literally not the same person you were a week ago or even yesterday! Every day, our bodies undergo many changes - some big, some small. How we look on the outside is constantly changing, but so is everything on the inside.

One look at mother nature proves this is just par for the course. The weather is always changing, sometimes minute by minute and sometimes day to day. The Earth's landscape continuously evolves, with mountains eroding over time and new ones forming. The trees in your backyard constantly grow and morph as new leaves and branches form. The frog would be a good example of change because it goes through many different stages in its life - from tadpole to adult. And then you have the timeless example of the caterpillar, making its ultimate transformation into: a *flying* creature.

The entire way of the Universe is expansion - therefore, nothing ever stays the same.

It would be easy to acknowledge this fact and instantly feel scared, small, and alone. But, just *what if* - you embraced it? What if you saw change as something exciting and beautiful instead of something to be afraid of?

 *"Life is a process of becoming, a combination of states we have to go through. Where people fail is that they wish to elect a state and remain in it. This is a kind of death."*

— ANAIS NIN

Anais Nin was onto something there. The key is to avoid trying to stay in any *one* state - including how our bodies look. Change is inevitable - whether we like it or not.

I'm not saying that you should actively seek change or strive for it in your life. However, I am saying that you should be open to it and accept it when it happens.

The best way to deal with change is to *go with the flow.* Let's use a pimple as an ironic example. Say you get a pimple on your nose (a true challenge). Instead of getting all worked up about it, just let it be. Pimples are a natural part of life, and they go away eventually. If you start picking at them, they will only take longer to heal and could leave behind **scars**. Don't give your new pimple too much attention or energy; maybe even crack a joke before someone else does, and then let change take its course as it disappears. (Pimples really are the worst, though. Maybe this wasn't the best example.)

The same goes for our bodies in general. If we can learn to go with the flow, then we will be happier, more confident, and better equipped to deal with the changes that do occur. Accept the temporary, undesired side-effects as natural change, don't empower them by "picking" at them, and let them go as quickly as they came.

Quick tips for going with the flow:

- Be *open* to change. Resisting or fighting it only makes things harder and never serves you.
- Be flexible. Be willing to adjust your "plans" or mindset based on the changes that may come up.
- Let go of control. Remember - you can't control *anything* except your thoughts and actions.
- Trust yourself. You have the ability to handle whatever changes come your way.
- Have faith. Everything happens for a reason, even if we don't understand it at the time.

You're turning into an adult. It all just makes sense when you put it into perspective - it's even pretty cool. Do you honestly think you are strange because you're "changing"? Show me someone who's NOT changing. Then I'll be truly freaked out.

Although accepting change is a big part of developing a positive body image, you'll still need to be more proactive. So how can we learn to *love* and accept our bodies just as they are?

PRACTICING SELF-LOVE

 *"To love oneself is the beginning of a lifelong romance."*

— OSCAR WILDE

Self-love is not about being arrogant or thinking too highly of oneself but about accepting oneself for who one is. Loving yourself seems like it should be easy, but for many people, it's not. We are often our own worst critics and can be very hard on ourselves. This is especially true when it comes to our bodies.

The first step is recognizing that you ARE worthy of love and respect - just as you are. You don't need to lose 10 pounds, get a new wardrobe, or achieve any other "goal" before you can start loving yourself. Those things will only be easier to accomplish once you DO love yourself.

Combining my own experience, experiences with my children, and extensive research, I'd like to offer some solid methods for you to begin practicing self-love *now*.

ACCEPT COMPLIMENTS AND PRAISE FROM OTHERS

I have a confession - I used to HATE when people complimented me. It would make me uncomfortable, and I would usually brush it off or say something self-deprecating to divert the attention. Can you relate?

The thing is, when we don't accept compliments, we reject the love and positive energy that the other person is trying to send our way. By not taking their praise, we indirectly tell ourselves, "That's not true."

It can be hard to break this habit, but it's important to try. The next time someone tells you they like your style, smile, or hair - maybe take a deep breath and say, "Thank you." Feel the words as you say them, and let the positive energy of the praise fill you up. You have to decide to start letting self-love develop at some point. Allowing others to help you there is an excellent path of least resistance!

MINDFUL MOVEMENT

You've probably heard a million times that exercise is great for physical and mental health. And this is undoubtedly true - it's like a miracle drug! It keeps your heart healthy, helps control weight, increases endorphins (or "happy hormones"), promotes good sleep, and reduces the risk of depression while boosting self-esteem (Kirby 2019). So yes - do the exercise! But what I mean by "mindful movement" goes even deeper than this.

How you carry yourself and the *way* you move your body can affect how you feel about yourself. Have you ever paid attention to the way you stand, the way you walk, and your posture? What about your hand movements or facial expressions?

Often, our level of self-love is reflected by our bodies. We can likewise affect our self-love by being conscious of our movement.

Once I attended a yoga class, and the teacher said something that stuck with me. She said, "When you move your body, you're moving your soul." That caused a lightbulb to go off in my head - the body really *is* a direct expression of what's inside. Unfortunately, until you realize this, sometimes it can act *against* you rather than *for* you.

If we make an effort to sit or stand up straight, with our shoulders back and chest out - we will naturally begin to feel more confident. We can also try smiling more, even if we don't "feel like it." Try using your hands and eyes when describing something you're passionate about. The mind is highly intuitive, and these simple changes in posture and movement can profoundly affect how we feel about ourselves.

You don't need to become over-animated. Just pay more attention and "practice until you perfect it." How does the best version of you *move*? Like you don't want to be there? Or alive and full of energy? Remember - it's a self-fulfilling prophecy.

SPEND TIME IN FRONT OF THE MIRROR

Mirrors don't only show us how we look on the outside - they can also be reflective of our emotions and help us see hidden aspects of ourselves.

This may seem odd, but I challenge you to spend at least five minutes in front of the mirror every day looking at yourself. Awkward and vain as it may feel, it's essential to get comfortable with your reflection. How can you love yourself if you don't even know what you truly look like?

Don't just zoom in on the physical imperfections - although it's important to love those too. Take note of your best features, the things you like about yourself. Again, I challenge you to find something every day that you appreciate about yourself and *focus on it*. Compliment yourself aloud if you have to - believe what you're saying.

Although it might seem silly, it's a great way to develop self-love. You are the only person who can truly appreciate your unique beauty, and once you learn to see yourself through your own eyes, the world will look at you differently, too. But don't be surprised if you experience side effects, such as: learning to remain present with yourself, managing your feelings, and finding newfound inner strength.

TAKE CARE OF YOUR BODY

This one is SO obvious, right? Wrong - you would be shocked to learn how many people *do not care for themselves*.

By "take care of your body," I mean: proper sleep, eating, drinking, hygiene, etc.

How do you treat a new pet that you love? Your car or bike? Your girlfriend or boyfriend that you are crazy about? You take care of them. You've got to start caring about your body the same way. Well, *more*.

I'm not trying to insult your intelligence - I know you know this stuff! Skipping out on sleep can lead to mood swings, irritability, and poor academic performance. There are many delicious *and* nutritious foods - find a balance for your body's needs. Don't fill your body with garbage (junk food, soda, alcohol, smoking whatever you smoke). Take showers. Brush your dang teeth!!

These are the basics, friends - but you have to DO them. Remember "GIGO" or - "Garbage In, Garbage Out." "You are what you eat" works, too. If you put clean, healthy things into your body - it will treat you nicely in return. But if you neglect your body, don't be surprised when it starts breaking down on you - and you begin to resent it in return.

LIMIT SOCIAL MEDIA

You can't always control what types of people you are around or what situations you find yourself in. There will always be someone or something to compare yourself to. You DO, however, have direct control over your social media usage.

Now, I'm not advising you to eliminate all your accounts. I wouldn't dare - I love social media for many reasons! But we all know that it can be a big time-waster and sometimes even detrimental to our mental health.

If you constantly compare your life to others on social media, it's probably time to look closer. Scroll through your feed and note how you feel after viewing certain posts. Do they make you happy? Motivated? Jealous or resentful?

Think about why you are using social media in the first place. Is it to connect with friends and family? To follow your favorite celebrities or brands? To show off your own life?

There's nothing wrong with any of those things, but if you find that social media is making you feel bad about yourself more often than not, it might be time to take a break. Or at least make a conscious effort to limit your use. I have to make this decision every once in a while, and I can say that it usually ends up being very refreshing. Typically, after a hiatus, I don't crave it as much when I return to it.

Believe it or not, this is a form of self-love. That's because you're choosing to put yourself **first**, refusing to succumb to the temptation of something you know may not be the best for your mental health or body image.

START A GRATITUDE JOURNAL

Journaling is **great** because it gives you space to get your feelings out. It allows you to vent, develop coping abilities, and empower yourself.

Gratitude (which we will explore further in chapter nine) is one of the keys to a great life. The more gratitude you feel, the more you are given to feel grateful for.

These two things make a winning combination! A real PB & J. They're like cookies and milk. Spaghetti and meatballs. Chips and guacamole. Burger and fries…

This is NOT the direction I wanted to go after advising you to limit junk food. But you get the point - it's a good combo.

A gratitude journal can be as simple as a small notebook kept by your bed or on your nightstand. Some suggest writing three to five things you are grateful for every night. Well, I say go crazy with it. Just do a "brain dump" of everything you're thankful for every morning *and* night!

I can think of a million things on the spot right NOW - my health, the health of my family and loved ones, a secure home to live in, freedom to travel and go on adventures, my cats, a beautiful planet to live on, technology…the list can go on forever.

And since we're currently focusing on body image and self-love, be sure to include that! What about your ability to walk and run, your eyesight, maybe you like your height or your arms or teeth? We take many things for granted that other people would trade *anything* for. Writing it down makes it more real, and don't forget - what you focus your attention on *expands*.

JEALOUSY

Jealousy is a complex emotion that is also in complete opposition to self-love. It's one of the most toxic and harmful emotions that a person can experience.

With a jealous mindset, you will always find someone "better" than you. It will never end. Regarding body image, it's simply impossible to be happy and content with yourself when you're always focused on the qualities of others.

Jealousy is not to be confused with admiration. Admiration is when you see someone doing something or possessing something you would like for yourself, and it motivates you to achieve your goals. Jealousy is when you see someone with something you want, and it makes you resentful and angry.

Often, people can be jealous of others without even realizing it. It's crucial to catch these feelings early on, so they don't spiral out of control.

Remember everything we've practiced leading up to this point:

1. You never know what other people are thinking - they are probably just as jealous of someone else as you might be of them.
2. Your unique qualities are always going to be what make you a potential **leader**.
3. Practicing confidence in walking, talking, and moving will *always* make you attractive.

4. Focusing on what you like and love about yourself will reflect that reality in the outside world.

Your physical beauty is, and will always be, the shallowest aspect of your beauty. While you should accept, love, nurture, and embrace your physical self, remember that you are SO much more. Because once you do, everyone else will follow.

Create Your Life (Chapter 6)

This chapter is about something that affects everyone—your body. Or more specifically, how you *feel* about your body. Let's be real: learning to accept and love how you look isn't always easy. But it is possible—and powerful.

Use this section to reflect honestly, shift negative thoughts, and build a better relationship with your body.

WHAT DO YOU USUALLY THINK WHEN YOU LOOK IN THE MIRROR?

How true are those thoughts?

_____

_____

_____

_____

_____

_____

_____

_____

_____

_____

☞ LIST THREE THINGS YOU LIKE ABOUT YOUR BODY—EVEN IF THEY'RE SMALL OR WEIRD.

_____

_____

_____

_____

_____

_____

_____

_____

_____

_____

■ HOW DOES SOCIAL MEDIA AFFECT THE WAY YOU FEEL ABOUT YOUR
APPEARANCE? BE HONEST.

_____

_____

_____

_____

_____

_____

_____

_____

_____

_____

HOW DO PEOPLE AROUND YOU TALK ABOUT THEIR OWN BODIES—AND HOW DOES IT AFFECT YOU?

_____

_____

_____

_____

_____

_____

_____

_____

_____

_____

WHAT WOULD CHANGE IF YOU STOPPED COMPARING YOURSELF TO
OTHERS FOR JUST ONE WEEK?

_____

_____

_____

_____

_____

_____

_____

_____

_____

_____

7

THE SECOND "B" WORD

I'll be honest - bullies remain one of my biggest triggers to this day. Although bullying comes in many forms and continues throughout life, a bullied child is the ONE thing that tugs at my heartstrings the most. For a teenager, being bullied is a surefire way to have your self-confidence destroyed completely.

I was bullied throughout middle school and part of high school. But I've also seen the effects of bullying on others, and I fear for it in my children's lives. How can one human be so heartless as to tear down and ruin another? I never understood it.

Allow me to "reminisce" some more...

As cliche as it may sound, school lunch was the worst for me. As soon as I finally found a few people to share a table with, we became one giant target. Other groups would surround us with their tables every day, throwing food and other objects. They did their best to make that half hour utterly miserable for the four or five of us. I'm assuming it was because we weren't in any specific "clique" - we were simply loners being lonely together.

Oddly enough, it didn't bother me so much anymore that *I* was being picked on - I'd gotten pretty good at blocking others out. What made me *angry* was seeing my new friends being harassed. "WHY?" I would ask myself. These were pretty good kids once you got to know them. Talented, funny, and intelligent. What gave someone else the right to hurt another human so deeply - more deeply than they could ever possibly know?

And then, after the anger, came the hopelessness. "What could I *do*?". Therein lies the major frustration with bullying: what *can* you do?

The word "bully" can be defined as "a person or people who intimidate or ridicule an individual with the intent of hurting them physically or emotionally" - and it's a tricky, complex situation. There is often more to it than meets the eye.

We can break down the components of bullying into three parts: the victim, the bully, and the bystander. At some point, you may have been any one of the three. Regardless of your role, your mission is to learn, heal, and overcome bullying - then empower others.

Regarding school and cyberbullying in 2022

- About 20% of U.S. students aged 12 to 18 are bullied during the school year.
- At 79%, verbal harassment is the most common type of bullying at school.
- Sixth-graders experience the most bullying, at 31%.
- 29% of middle school students have been bullied in the classroom.
- 64% of young adults have been bullied by a teacher at least once.
- In 30% of the cases among 12 to 18-year-old students, bullying is related to physical appearance.
- 70.4% of school staff have witnessed bullying.
- Since January 2021, 41% of U.S. internet users have experienced some form of cyberbullying.
- One-fifth of bullying happens on social media.
- Rude name-calling is the most common form of child cyberbullying, at 42%.
- 37% of teens are bullied online before they turn 18.

(What To Become 2022)

THE VICTIM

When most people think of bullying, they first picture the victim. Victims are often targeted because they are different in some way or weaker than the bully. They may be smaller, shy, disabled, or have a different skin color or religion. Bullies use their perceived "power" to control and humiliate their victims.

Bullying can take many forms, but it *always* harms the victim. Physical bullying can involve hitting, punching, slapping, or any other type of physical violence. Emotional bullying can include teasing, name-calling, threatening, gossiping, and spreading rumors. Cyberbullying is when it takes place online - through social media, texts, or emails. All types of bullying can leave the victim feeling alone, scared, and vulnerable.

Unfortunately, victims of bullying can also experience much more severe repercussions. They may develop anxiety, depression, or other mental health disorders. They could experience fatigue, poor academic performance, and higher dropout rates. And in the worst cases, victims may harm themselves or attempt suicide.

So, *what can victims do?* It's important again to remember that you are not alone, and there are people who can help. You have options. Although *all* of these may not be appropriate to your situation, here are some steps to take if you find yourself in the role of the victim:

1. **Understand.** This may very well be the most difficult. You must mentally understand, and KNOW, that the problem is the bully - not you. If you believe the bully's actions and words, moving on will become very tough. Remember this: people can only love from *their level of self-love.* In hurting others, it is most likely that a bully has unresolved issues with him or herself, deals with trauma, or has been the victim in another circumstance. If you are a victim, the last thing you want to be told is to have empathy. Well, you don't have to forgive the bully just yet - but you must forgive yourself.

2. **Speak up.** I know (trust me) - this is hard, too. But it would be best if you told someone about the bullying. It could be a parent, teacher, counselor, trusted adult, or at the very least - a friend. Telling someone can help you feel better and may also put an end to the problem. It is most important to get the attention of a trusted adult because they are best equipped with the experience and resources to deal with this sensitive situation. If you've told someone and they took no action - **persist.** DON'T STOP until you have the full attention of at least one qualified adult and they are *doing* something about it.

3. **Ignore the bully.** It can be challenging, but ignoring the bully can sometimes be the best way to stop them. Bullies are looking for a reaction - if you don't give them one, they may get bored and move on. Again, you will have to use your discretion in the matter. Avoidance could be a great option if it is a "general" bully who kind of picks on everyone. This might not be the most successful strategy if they are mainly focused on *you* - or, for example, they're on your bus every day.

4. **Stand up for yourself.** If you can do it safely - stand up to the bully. This takes courage, but it may show the bully that you are not an easy target. Remember one thing, though: be assertive, not aggressive. The point is not to fuel the situation but

to stop it. In some instances, a bully might not even fully recognize the level to which they're affecting you. Their *definition* of bullying might be slightly different from yours. If this feels like it might be the case, try pulling them aside and saying, "Do you mind if we talk for a minute...?" while expressing how they are making you feel. Calmly asserting your point of view and being open may just do the trick.

5. **Build allies.** This is a great one, which I recommend regardless of the situation. Find peers or friends who will be on your side to make you feel more supported, connected, and confident. You'll want to make a deal with these people, saying, "If I'm being picked on, you stand up for me - and I'll do the same for you." There is strength in numbers, and most bullies won't have the desire or motivation to stand up to a group.

6. **Block the bully online.** Whether you are being cyberbullied or physically bullied, be sure to block the person doing it. You can also report their behavior to social media sites. This one is a little obvious, and it's not the end-all in most cases - but it's definitely a step that needs to be taken to safeguard yourself from every form of harmful contact.

THE BULLY

The bully is not a one-dimensional person. There are different types of bullies with different motivations. Some do it to feel powerful, and some do it for attention. Others may do it because, as previously mentioned, they are or have been victims of bullying. No matter the reason, bullying is **still harmful** to everyone involved.

Yes, it is often hard to see from the eyes of a bully or to have any compassion *at all*. But what if, for just a moment, we tried? And if you're the bully, have you asked yourself *why*?

I often have to remind myself that when it comes down to it, we all want the same thing - to be happy. This in no way excuses or justifies bullying. But *understanding* will undoubtedly bring a level of relief and possible resolution for both the victim and the bully.

"People who love themselves, don't hurt other people. The more we hate ourselves, the more we want others to suffer."

— DAN PEARCE

Bullies are often people with low self-esteem who feel powerless in other areas of their lives. Does this resonate with you? You may be acting out because you are experiencing some sort of pain, and lashing out is your way of coping.

Often, bullying can be a learned behavior. Maybe you've witnessed someone being bullied in the past and thought it was funny or compelling. Perhaps you're doing it to get attention or show off. This is another sign of *diminished* self-love and, believe it or not, false self-confidence.

It's important to note that not all bullies are bad people, even though they are causing harm. Do you currently classify as a bully? Take a good look. **What can the bully do** to overcome?

1. **The Golden Rule.** That's right - *treat others the way you want to be treated.* It's simple - take a step back and put yourself in the victim's shoes. How would you feel if the roles were reversed? This will help you develop empathy and realize that your actions are wrong. Want to take it a step further? *Try standing up for victims.* You can instantly change your role this way. You can also start to feel much better about yourself (just don't bully the other bullies)!

2. **Understand the effects.** It's important to realize that your actions have consequences. When you bully someone, it not only affects them, but it also affects you and the people around you. The whole thing is a lose-lose situation. We've gone over the effects on the victim, but what about the impact on the *bully*? Bullies often have difficulty making friends and forming relationships. This is because most people don't want to associate with someone who is mean and aggressive. As a result, bullies can often feel isolated and alone. They also typically run a greater risk of drinking, smoking, doing drugs, having negative attitudes, and performing poorly in school. Ultimately, bullies tend to go down dangerous roads - sometimes getting involved with sketchy people and situations, psychiatric disorders, and trouble with the law (Styx 2021). This is likely because they learn that violence and aggression are acceptable ways to get what they want.

3. **Know the difference between teasing and bullying.** You *must* be able to distinguish between the two. Teasing is done in a good-natured way, usually involving friends and with the intention of making someone laugh. Bullying is done with the intention of causing harm and is often done by people who are not friends with the victim. There is a hard line between the two - don't cross it. If someone looks like they're no longer having a good time, *stop*. If someone asks you to stop, *stop*.

4. **Find the root cause.** It's easier said than done, but try to get to the bottom of things. What's causing you to act this way? Are you feeling insecure in other areas? Is there something going on at home that's making you act out? There's always a motivating reason that lies beneath the surface. Once you identify the root cause, you can start to address it. This will be a crucial step in overcoming your behavior.

5. **Channel your energy.** If you're angry or frustrated, try finding a positive outlet for that energy. It can be anything from sports to creative endeavors. The key is to discover something that makes you feel good and allows you to express your *good* qualities. You may be surprised to see how doing so could change your outlook on life. Chapter five is *all* about this!

6. **Seek help.** If you're struggling to figure yourself out on your own, talking with somebody else can be a good idea. Finding a safe person to speak with may quickly help solutions arise. If that doesn't work and you feel like your condition is more extreme, it may be time to seek professional help. A therapist or counselor can help you understand the root cause of your behavior and develop a plan to change it. You may even find relief in a support group of similar people. There is no shame in seeking help - in fact, it takes a lot of strength and courage.

THE BYSTANDER

"If you turn and face the other way when someone is being bullied, you might as well be the bully too."

— UNKNOWN

The third part of the bullying equation, which is often overlooked, is that of the bystander. The ironic part about being outside of the situation is that they are potentially in the best position to help the victim - but they can also be part of the problem. Bystanders have a choice: encourage the bully or stand up to them. Often, they may be scared of getting involved or need help figuring out what to do.

More likely than not, we've *all* been the bystander at some point. It's easy to feel helpless in these situations, but you have more power than you realize - there are things you can do to make a difference. And speaking from experience, it is *not fun* living with the guilt of knowing you could've helped someone who needed it or missed out on an opportunity to do something extraordinary.

What are your powers as the bystander?

1. **Get verbal.** The first and most important thing you can do is *say something*. This can go a long, long way in diffusing a bad situation. It can be as simple as "That's not cool, stop it" or "Leave them alone." You don't have to be best friends with the victim to stand up for them - sometimes, it means *more* coming from a stranger. Simply showing support this way aids the victim without encouraging things to get physical or dangerous. If it does get physical, **scream** if you have to. No shame. Your intervention may very well prevent the situation from escalating or happening again.

2. **Get help.** If possible, you should find a teacher or adult who can aid in the situation effectively, especially if someone's safety is at hand. This will minimize the chance of escalation, provide relief for the victim, and hold the bully accountable for their actions. Victims will often be too scared or embarrassed to speak up for themselves. Make sure that the adult is dealing with this in the long term, not just scolding the bully and walking away. "The squeaky wheel gets the grease." That means the more you insist that serious action is taken, the better chance it will get done. Remember - reporting the bully is not "tattling." It is the responsible thing to do, and it is for the greatest good.

3. **Show support.** After the situation has diffused, the victim will likely feel scared, helpless, or embarrassed. This is a moment to show them that they are not alone - that there are people who care about them. Be friendly, and let them know you're there for them if they need to talk. For instance, you could say, "Hey, are you okay? That looked pretty rough back there. Do you want to talk about it?" This could make all the difference in helping somebody who is struggling. It serves as a reminder that there is someone in their corner.

The bystander role is a unique but important one. You have the opportunity to make a **real** difference in somebody's life and to prevent further harm from coming their way.

Create Your Life (Chapter 7)

Whether you've been a victim, a bystander, or the one causing harm, this chapter is about honesty, healing, and growth. Bullying is a complex topic, but reflection and awareness can begin to shift everything. Let's take a deeper look.

HAVE YOU EVER BEEN BULLIED?

How did it affect you then—and how does it still affect you now? (If you haven't, you can use a situation involving someone else as an example.)

_____

_____

_____

_____

_____

_____

_____

_____

_____

WHAT DO YOU WISH SOMEONE HAD DONE TO HELP YOU?

(Or to help someone else?)

_____

_____

_____

_____

_____

_____

_____

_____

_____

HAVE YOU EVER BEEN UNKIND IN A WAY THAT MIGHT HAVE FELT LIKE BULLYING TO SOMEONE ELSE? WHY DO YOU THINK THAT HAPPENED?

_____

_____

_____

_____

_____

_____

_____

_____

_____

IF YOU COULD GO BACK AND SPEAK TO YOURSELF DURING THAT TIME, WHAT WOULD YOU SAY?

_____

_____

_____

_____

_____

_____

_____

_____

_____

HAVE YOU EVER STOOD UP FOR SOMEONE ELSE?

If yes, how did it feel? If not, what held you back?

_____

_____

_____

_____

_____

_____

_____

_____

_____

_____

8

RULER OF YOUR KINGDOM

Being a shameless fantasy junkie myself, I would like to share a story of two kingdoms - both of which couldn't be more different from one another - and their rulers, who experienced two very different fates...

The Queen

The first kingdom was ruled by a sage and loving queen. She was revered by her subjects, who trusted that she made good decisions regarding their protection, dealing with advisors, and maintaining a fair and just society.

When it came to defense, no expense was spared. Only the finest stone, clay, and wood fortified the castle walls. Covering every inch of the grounds' perimeter, they stood a breathtaking 40 feet tall in some spots and measured 15 feet thick. It is rumored that the sight of the walls alone was enough to intimidate and drive away the queen's most dangerous enemies.

Throughout her reign, only the top barons, lords, bishops, and close family members were allowed inside the Queen's Chamber. This innermost sanctum was her domain - a place where her council could meet without interference or distraction. Knowing that the matters discussed here were of utmost importance, each person who entered swore an oath of secrecy. The queen was cautious about the people she surrounded herself with. While some were born into nobility, others had to earn their place through acts of bravery or by proving their worth in other ways. She believed that it was essential to have a variety of voices at her table; however, the queen's word was always final.

Ultimately, this wise queen knew her success was only as great as the success of her kingdom as a whole. She believed in leading by example and inspiring others. Upon seeing her subjects struggling, she quickly offered her hand. This kindness was often reciprocated and resulted in a strong sense of community. People were proud to belong to this kingdom.

These qualities, alongside many others, caused peace to flourish for many years. The people were happy, and the land prospered. As legend has it, the queen's rule was so loved and admired that other kingdoms began to emulate her ways. The foundations she established caused prosperity to carry on long after she was gone, providing a legacy that would continue for generations.

The King

An egotistical and narcissistic king ruled the second kingdom. He was either feared or loathed by his subjects - or some combination of the two. It was well known that the king often made careless decisions without considering the consequences.

This shortsighted ruler was more concerned with luxury and impressing others than protecting his kingdom and people. Rather than fortifying the structures, walls, and houses, the king spent money on lavish jewelry, entertainment, and an excess of food. Shortcuts were made constantly, which showed as weather and invaders slowly began to chip away at the kingdom's resources.

This king surrounded himself with "yes men" - people who would always agree with him, no matter what, strengthening his egoic sense of power. Without honest feedback or constructive criticism, the king was free to do whatever he wanted, no matter how foolish it might be.

As the king became increasingly wrapped up in false appearances, exorbitance, and gratification, it was no surprise that others were soon able to take advantage of him. He began to be led astray by supposed "wise men" from all over - snakes disguised as allies, seeking to exploit his weaknesses. They fed his ego with compliments and convinced him to make poor decisions that would benefit them, all while putting his kingdom at risk.

It became harder and harder to counteract all the misfortune this kingdom experienced. In weak efforts to do so, the desperate king would raise taxes without warning or start foolish wars that left many people dead or wounded. He became known to be quite manipulative, often using others to get what he wanted and discarding them when he was done.

As you can imagine, the king's recklessness and lack of concern for what mattered eventually led to the downfall of his kingdom. Just as quickly as it rose, it crumbled - leaving behind a wake of destruction and a dismal legacy.

THE CASTLE WALLS

It doesn't matter if you are a king, a queen, a dog, or a cat - in any case, **you** are the ruler of your kingdom. Your kingdom is your scope of influence, your "circle," your people - and every decision you make regarding **who you let in** will affect it.

The castle walls represent the **boundaries** you set to protect yourself from being harmed, misled, or taken advantage of.

Your boundaries, or walls, will show others (and yourself) who you are, how you want to be treated, and what is important to you. If your walls are weak, others will quickly enter your "kingdom" and take control. On the other hand, if your walls are strong, it will be much harder for others to get in, and you'll have much more authority over who and what influences you.

Although your boundaries have the ability to block out some influences completely, they also have the power to create **space**. This space can protect you from physical and mental harm when it comes to acquaintances, friends, dating partners, certain adults, and the digital world.

WHEN SHOULD YOU SET BOUNDARIES?

The simple answer is: whenever you need to.

But it's not always that simple, especially if you've never practiced it. Understand that generally, feelings of *discomfort* will signify that a situation may be unhealthy and a boundary is needed.

Consider using a **1-5 scale of "sensitivity,"** with a one being completely harmless and a five being very harmful. The point is to determine where specific people and things in your life fall on this scale. You could ask yourself these questions to determine the number:

- Do you feel safe in this situation/with this person?
- Do you feel like you're being heard?
- Do you feel like you're being respected?
- Do you feel like you need help in dealing with it/them?

Here are some examples to show how your feelings can be a guide to your boundaries:

1. You have a friend on the bus who is a grade below you and really looks up to you. Every morning you get on the bus, they beg you to sit next to them - but love to talk your ear off. It may be a bit annoying sometimes, but 1) it's a safe situation, 2) you're being heard and respected, and 3) it's nothing you can't handle on your own. You might give this a "1" on the scale - it's pretty harmless.

2. A group of kids at school use each other to cheat on tests. They are generally nice kids, but you know their actions aren't right. They have asked you if you'd like to get in on it - but that's not for you. Using the questions above, you determine 1) it's relatively "safe," although not morally right. 2) You're being heard and respected because you said "no" to their offer, and they've dropped it for now. 3) If it persists, you may need to involve someone else (like a teacher). You might rate this situation a 2-3, knowing you need to create some space (we'll talk about "how" shortly).

3. You've been dating for about a month, and your boyfriend or girlfriend is "bored" with just kissing. They are putting some light pressure on you to spend time together alone. Being young and still a bit unsure, you don't feel overly safe in that situation - you're not mentally prepared for it. You may also need to talk to your parents or a trusted relative for some advice. You put this at a "3," knowing that you need to ensure you're both on the same page and that things are moving along at the right pace.

4. You find yourself a bystander in a bullying situation. A few kids you consider "friends" are involved, encouraging the bully and also encouraging you to join in. Although you aren't in direct harm, this situation doesn't feel safe. You don't feel respected because they tease you when you don't join. You probably also need a teacher to get involved at this point. So, you put these "friends" at a 4. Time to create some significant distance and, if they don't change, consider putting some serious boundaries up.

5. There is a game you love playing online, but it's developing a bad reputation. Parents are starting to discover that many predators are playing this game, posing as kids. One day, someone approaches you in a chat room on the game, asking some very personal and odd questions. 1) This is NOT safe. 2) You feel

disrespected and a bit confused. 3) You feel strange and need to tell your parents about what happened. This would be a "5" on the scale. It's best to put up a *hard wall*, delete the game, and report it.

HOW SHOULD YOU SET BOUNDARIES?

Once you've used your feelings to determine the severity of a situation, what do you do about it? The type of boundary you set should be appropriate to the number you've assigned. Going back to our scale, here are some suggestions:

1 - 2 on the scale) You should establish some physical space. This might mean sitting far away from the person on the bus (if it gets overbearing). It might mean being upfront with the group of kids cheating, saying something like "No thanks, I don't feel good about this," and then keeping a healthy distance from them in the future. In any regard, setting boundaries means being **clear and direct**. It's about *not wavering* in your decision or caving into the pressure of the moment.

3 - 4 on the scale) Now you may need to put up some emotional space as well. It would be best to spend less time with this person or situation and set clear verbal guidelines. It may be time to approach an adult for help as well. Going back to the cheating kids: if the situation escalates and they continue to approach you, you should consult your parents and a teacher for advice. For the boyfriend or girlfriend who wants to take things further, you'll want to make sure your stance is well-understood and respected. Maybe say, "I care about you a lot, but I don't want to feel pressured into anything I'm not ready for - mutual consent needs to be our main focus." And for the bully situation, it might be time to stop considering these people your "friends." Let them know that you are entirely against picking on others and that no friends of yours would treat another this way. Avoid them as much as possible, block them on social media or delete their numbers from your phone.

5 on the scale) You will most likely want to put up a hard boundary. It would be best if you told your parents, teachers, or even the police, in extreme cases. Hypothetically speaking, you should delete the app or game, block the person from ever contacting you again, and avoid the situation at all costs.

It's not always easy to set boundaries, but doing what feels *right* for you is necessary. You can always change your boundaries if needed - they are not necessarily set in stone. And remember, it's OK to be selfish when it comes to your well-being!

THE COUNCIL

"A mirror reflects a man's face, but what he is really like is shown by the kind of friends he chooses."

— COLIN POWELL

As you get good at setting boundaries and creating healthy space from toxicity, you'll naturally want to fill that space up with the *opposite*. Just as a king or queen needs a competent and trusted council to help rule the kingdom, teenagers need positive and respected influencers to help them grow in confidence and better themselves. As you know, not all influences are great. So, how do you choose the best ones?

Here are some questions to ask yourself when considering someone a potential "influencer":

- Do they make you feel good about yourself?
- Do they encourage and support your dreams and ambitions?
- Do they help you grow as a person?
- Do they fit YOUR vision of the world?

Sticking with the kingdom analogy, think of it like this:

The **villagers** on the outskirts of the kingdom represent your **acquaintances or peers**. These could be people you run into at the mall or the store. You might know them from school - you wave and are friendly with them but don't know too much about them beyond that. They might be people in your classes or even distant relatives you see from time to time. You don't necessarily have as much control over your peers, but they also don't carry as much weight.

Then you have the **people who live within the castle walls**. These are the **friends** you regularly associate with. In addition to your friends, these could include family members, teachers, and even role models (we'll expand on role models in a bit). As a general rule: the closer you let people in, the more impact they will have on your life.

Finally, you have the chamber room with your **advisors**. This is the most private of spaces, where the big decisions are made. These people will become the most influential and impactful people in your kingdom. "Advisors" may include your **best friend(s), your parents or family members, and anyone you trust, look up to and confide in**.

Be extremely cautious with *who* you allow in and how *close* you let them. It can take time to identify the right people, so remember to go slow and get to know someone before getting too involved. Just like you wouldn't let a stranger into your home without knowing them first, you shouldn't let just anyone into your inner circle.

An excellent way to test someone's character is by giving them a little power and seeing how they use it. For example, let's say you have a friend who always asks to borrow money from you. Consider lending them a small amount first, and see if they pay you back promptly as agreed upon. If they do, great - you can trust them with a little more power. If they don't, you know they might not be someone you can rely on. Can you devise more ways of "testing the water" with others, allowing you to progress slowly and securely with them?

One thing is for sure: you should never feel like you have to change yourself to fit someone else's idea of who you should be. As soon as that feeling creeps in - the feeling of not being **authentic** - it should raise a giant red flag. You should always be evolving on your terms, not someone else's. Your real friends will always be comfortable with you being YOU.

MEDIA INFLUENCERS

Pop stars, sports heroes, actors, actresses, YouTubers, social media "celebrities" - these are people that teenagers (and adults, too) all over the world look up to. It's natural for humans to put others on pedestals and to want to be like them somehow. You need to acknowledge (and control) the *level of importance* you place on them - that is the key.

Some people might say you should never look up to anyone because you will only ever be disappointed, but I think that's a bit of an extreme view. It's OK to have role models and people you admire - but try not to place your **self-worth** on them. If you start to find yourself wanting to be just like them - to the point where you begin to change your appearance, interests, and values - then it might be time to take a step back.

Also - and perhaps even more importantly - what image do your role models portray in their lives? Just like your "real life" influencers, you must ensure that the people you look up to display qualities you want to experience in YOUR world. If they're materialistic, violent, insensitive, or depict themselves negatively, remember that it will directly influence you to the **degree of importance you place upon them**.

So ask yourself this: do your role models make you feel good about yourself? And I mean the REAL you - the one you've been discovering throughout this book. Do they encourage your dreams and ambitions? Does their influence help you grow as a person? Take some time to learn about the people you're interested in - look up interviews, read their biographies, and get a feel for who they really are. See if they live their life in a way that you wholeheartedly relate to and have values that align with yours.

Just because someone is famous, or has a lot of money, doesn't mean they're a good role model. Media stars *especially* need to be taken with a grain of salt.

Regardless of what you may think, you don't know these role models as people - you only see them through the lens of their public persona. You see them through the decisions they've made to "sell" themselves and even decisions that are out of their hands - the ones determined by managers, labels, etc.! It's just not real life. Some of the most successful people in the world are also some of the most unhappy - and have made some pretty poor choices.

"Whoever controls the media, the images, controls the culture."

— ALLEN GINSBERG

As you get older, you might find that your role models change, and that's perfectly normal. Your values and priorities will also change as you learn more about yourself and the world around you. Just stay uniquely *you*, keep *yourself* at the center, and *don't be blinded* by appearances.

THE RISING TIDE

"A rising tide lifts all boats."

— JOHN F. KENNEDY

Although this quote has traditionally been used in politics regarding the economy, it couldn't be more relevant when talking about confidence, self-esteem, and positivity (while fitting the kingdom theme!). These qualities don't only benefit the individual - they have a ripple effect on those around them as well.

Remember - you're part of the council, too! And as the ruler, you set the tone for the *entire kingdom*. The queen in our story knew this - she wisely kept the morale high because she knew that a happy kingdom was a productive one.

Another quote I like to live by, which conveys a similar point, is The Three Musketeers' "All for one and one for all." What a fantastic way to live - knowing that you are giving your **best** to everyone and trusting that they are doing the same for you. You now know that you can create your own empowering beliefs. Let this be one of them - live by this motto for a bit, and watch all the miraculous ways it begins to manifest in your life.

When you become an encourager, you're not just making others' lives better - you're making your own life better. It creates that "positive feedback loop" of inspiration and motivation. I can say with honesty and sincerity that learning to be a more giving person will allow you to experience deep joy and satisfaction that you won't receive anywhere else.

How to Be an Encourager

1. **Make sure your cup (or chalice) is "overflowing."** I'm addressing this again because it needs to stick! This HAS to be number one because if you are not "full," what do you have to offer others? You can't give what you don't have, after all. This notion was something I struggled with for a long time. I was in a place of trying to improve, trying to be my best for others - but I wasn't giving myself the same treatment. I often felt run-down, short-tempered, and unappreciated because of it. If you're at this point in the book, you know the importance of self-love and care - so make sure you're practicing it!

2. **LISTEN!** If you want to be of encouragement, you need to be a good listener. We all need to feel heard and understood. This might not be easy if you're someone who loves to talk - but it's definitely worth the effort. People will respond much better to you when they feel like you're listening rather than just waiting for your turn to talk. Listening is *essential* to communication, and it's easy to forget in this fast-paced world. We often find ourselves looking at our phones or thinking about what we will say next. Do your best to be **present** in the moment, letting others know you're truly tuned in to them.

3. (Or, 2b) **Suspend judgment.** When listening to someone, it's important to put aside all judgment. It's tricky to do, especially if you don't agree with what they're saying. But remember, you're not trying to change their opinion - you're trying to understand where they're coming from. Try to be open-minded, and see things

from their perspective. It doesn't mean that you have to agree with them - but it's a good exercise in empathy, which is a vital quality for anyone in a leadership position. Offer support, not advice. Sometimes, people just need to vent - and that's okay! Strive to be the person who genuinely cares.

4. **Compliment.** A compliment can go a long way. It's amazing how one kind word can completely change someone's day. Look for the good in others, and let them know what you see. But again - be *genuine*. There's nothing worse than a fake, phony compliment. Not only can the other person see right through it, but you'll also start to feel icky about yourself. They say that insincere flattery is just manipulation in disguise. Instead, be honest and give *specific* compliments when you can. "You're amazing!" is good, but "I love the way you handled that situation" or "Your enthusiasm is contagious!" are even better.

5. **Smile and make eye contact.** This one is simple and effective. Smiling is such a natural way to show appreciation and warmth. You can practice this with pretty much anyone you come in contact with, not just your friends. When you smile, you immediately feel happier - and that happy energy is contagious. Making eye contact is another way to show interest and engagement. It's more challenging if you're shy, but again - well worth the effort. We all know people who constantly avoid you when they walk by or always look like they hate the world. No one wants to be around someone continually casting shadows or putting out negative vibes. Instead, strive to make subtle connections and *be the light!*

6. **Go out of your way to do something kind.** This could be anything from holding the door open for someone to picking up a coffee for a friend to volunteering your time to a worthy cause. It doesn't have to be big or expensive - it just has to come from a good place. Pay it forward as often as possible, and watch the excellent karma return to you. Included in this should be encouraging others to reach for *their* goals. If you know someone working hard to achieve something, get in their corner! Let them know that you believe in them. *See them as their best version*, just as (hopefully) you do for yourself. This kind of support is especially crucial for teenagers, who are still figuring out who they are and what they want to do with their lives. Besides, just like everything else on this list, it *feels* good. And isn't that what we want - to feel good about ourselves?

Once you take control of your leadership qualities, you'll be well on your way to "raising the tide" - harnessing the power to improve your life and the lives of those around you. So set the example, and watch as others follow in your footsteps. Your kingdom starts with you.

Create Your Life (Chapter 8)

Your life is your kingdom. Every decision you make about who you let in, what you allow, and what you stand for shapes that kingdom. Use this section to reflect on your personal power, boundaries, and the people who influence your world.

IF YOU ARE THE RULER OF YOUR OWN KINGDOM, WHAT KIND OF RULER DO YOU WANT TO BE? WHAT QUALITIES WOULD YOUR PEOPLE ADMIRE IN YOU?

_____

_____

_____

_____

_____

_____

_____

_____

_____

THINK ABOUT YOUR "CASTLE WALLS." WHAT BOUNDARIES DO YOU NEED TO STRENGTHEN IN YOUR LIFE RIGHT NOW?

_____

_____

_____

_____

_____

_____

_____

_____

_____

_____

WHO'S INSIDE YOUR CASTLE, CLOSE TO YOU, INFLUENCING YOUR CHOICES?

Are they helping your kingdom thrive?

_____

_____

_____

_____

_____

_____

_____

_____

_____

_____

DO YOU HAVE ANY MEDIA INFLUENCERS THAT YOU NEED TO REEVALUATE?

Do they make you feel inspired, or not good enough?

_____

_____

_____

_____

_____

_____

_____

_____

HOW CAN YOU "RAISE THE TIDE" FOR OTHERS AROUND YOU?

List ways you can be an encourager, even in small ways.

_____

_____

_____

_____

_____

_____

_____

_____

_____

9

THE NEW MINDSET

It was finally high school graduation. "I can't believe I made it here," I remember thinking over and over. It was a beautiful day outside. Parents, relatives, friends, teachers - even *pets* filled the guest seats. I looked out to see my mom, dad, and brother beaming. Which "me" were they proud of? I certainly wasn't the same person I was at the beginning of seventh grade.

Yet here we were at this ceremony. And throughout the seemingly endless array of inspirational speeches, stories, awards, and diplomas, I found **one** question looming: "*NOW* what?"

You may think, "This is a normal question for a high school graduate!" And yes - graduation *is* one of the most crucial points in a young person's life, as their whole journey into the "real world" lies ahead. But that day, I wasn't asking that question in this way. You see, I'd already made up my mind that I was going to be a rock star. In fact, our first tour was already scheduled, and our manager had big plans for the foreseeable future...

No, "Now what?" came from a different perspective: "*Now* what would I do without my friends?"

I gazed around me to see the hundreds of faces that had, over time, transformed from enemies to allies. This was the world that had become my new "normal." I glanced at Rory in the very back (where the tall people go) and quietly thanked him for the gift he didn't even know he'd given me. I saw the "boy I won't name," who went from plaguing me in the halls to playing Pogs (look it up) with me in study hall. I saw my first girlfriend, and I saw my second. I saw some of the best people I'd ever met, and I saw the person who remains my best friend to this day.

Yes, these were the same people I once saw as strangers, the people I was *afraid* of - until my scope of *what was possible* expanded. And that's when it hit - deja vu!

This moment of graduation was my *new* "starting a new school." It was time to leave my comfort zone again and embrace new challenges. The only difference was that now, I was **prepared**.

Somehow, over the past six years, I stumbled upon the formula. I had no blueprint, roadmap, or GPS to guide me. I made mistakes - *lots* of them. I bounced from one "failure" to another and overcame many painful lessons regarding my self-worth. But along the way, there were tiny victories - and these little victories kept me going.

I found my *passion* - the thing that drove me. And through this, although a little backward, I found *myself*. I conquered false beliefs about my body and rewrote false assumptions about my peers - choosing to see things in a way that supported the life **I** wanted. I tapped into the wellspring of my power, learned to lean into my intuition, and began to see limitless potential all around me. This was true **self-confidence** - and now there was nothing but unwritten pages ahead, waiting to be filled.

A LEVEL PLAYING FIELD

Please view this chapter as the icing on the cake. The cherry on top. The final layer of gloss over all the fantastic work you've done to get here. Because in this chapter, you get to see how all this "work" has positioned you for greatness.

This chapter is intended to give you a sense of accomplishment - solidifying and imprinting your brand-new way of thinking. Whether you realize it or not, even if it's ever so slight, you are a **new person** now. A person that YOU chose and will continue to choose.

Remember this: **an old mindset *cannot* produce a new outcome!** That said, you must understand that there is only ONE thing required for a person to create any change in their life and maintain the new mindset. *Just. One. Thing.* And that thing is a DECISION.

The simple decision to want better for yourself is ALL you need for unstoppable self-confidence, high levels of self-worth, and overall higher quality and depth of life. Despite anything you've ever heard, **no one** has any advantage over you in this regard. **The playing field is level**.

No, you don't need a wealthy upbringing or a famous last name. You don't need to be six feet tall with washboard abs and a perfect smile. You don't have to be the most popular girl in school, have the "right" connections, or even GO to the "right" school. None of that matters - not even a little bit.

"It is not in the stars to hold our destiny but in ourselves."

— WILLIAM SHAKESPEARE

Do you need a little more proof?

- J.K. Rowling was a single mother living on welfare when she wrote the first Harry Potter book. Rowling's determination was evident in her writing as she persevered through rejections from publishers.
- Walt Disney was told he "lacked imagination" and was fired from an early animation job, driving another company into bankruptcy. Even in the face of these odds, he continued to pursue his passion.
- Decca Records rejected the Beatles with the comment, "We don't like their sound, and guitar music is on the way out." At least four major recording companies rejected them at the beginning.
- Michael Jordan was cut from his high school basketball team and was *not* genetically predisposed to be a basketball player. Despite this, he constantly visualized and practiced intensely to become one of the best in the world.
- In high school, Angelina Jolie was constantly teased for having braces, pouty lips, and being too skinny. She was later told she was "too dark" to be a successful actress, amongst several other challenges. She went on to be, well, Angelina Jolie.
- Stephen Hawking was told he wouldn't live past his early 20's. Despite being diagnosed with a terminal illness, he lived to be 76 and is revered as one of the world's greatest scientists.
- Hellen Keller was both deaf and blind. Fighting against ALL odds, she still learned how to communicate and went on to become a world-renowned author and lecturer.

Shall I go on? I think you get the point: as long as you maintain your **decision** to want better for yourself - *to be the authority of your mind* - there is NOTHING that can stop you from becoming the person you want to be and living the life you want to live. Don't let yourself believe that you are "not worthy" because now you know that is a *lie*! Although it may require your dedication, courage, and some work - not even the *work* will feel like work if you remain firm in your decision and your end goal (more about goals coming in a bit).

THE KEYS TO THE KINGDOM: ATTITUDE & GRATITUDE

I call them "keys" because your attitude and levels of gratitude allow you to open doors, lock them, and move around freely in your new domain. Without these keys in your pocket, what good is your kingdom?

No offense, but you might as well go ahead and throw away everything you've learned so far if your attitude is garbage. No one is perfect, obviously. And some people even find it very hard to be happy. But ask yourself: *"Does my attitude match my vision?"*

A bad attitude will single-handedly destroy your self-confidence, motivation, and happiness - no matter HOW MUCH knowledge you have about a topic. On the other hand, a good attitude will make you highly motivated and genuinely happy - no matter HOW LITTLE knowledge you have about a topic. Expressing enthusiasm will make it almost **impossible** for you to fail at *anything* you do.

To put it simply: A positive attitude trumps knowledge EVERY single time.

The good news is that your attitude is something that you can 100% control. You are the only one who can decide whether you will have a good day or a bad one. You're also the only one who can choose to focus on the positive or negative things in your life. I encourage you to remember and always keep in mind chapter three and the power of perception.

GRATITUDE

The sooner you understand the power of gratitude, the better. If someone asked me to summarize the secret of life in one word - well, this would be it.

I only WISH I was handed the knowledge of this precious key ten years sooner in my life. It would have saved me from a lot of unnecessary pain, suffering, and heartache (not that I regret anything!).

Gratitude is like a magical elixir that makes you feel happy, no matter what might be happening. It's also like superglue - it can fix almost any relationship (including the one you have with yourself). You can even feel grateful for things that *haven't* yet manifested.

And here's why it works: feeling grateful puts you in the vibration of *already* having the thing you are thankful for. There is no way to lose with gratitude. As your old reality cycles out and you hold onto this new attitude, everything that doesn't match it will wash away. Over time (and sometimes quite quickly), it will essentially "starve" the negative so it can no longer survive.

The best part? Gratitude is incredibly easy to cultivate. You can practice it anywhere, anytime - and it's 100% free. Go ahead and give it a try right now. Take a look around you. Start *feeling* grateful for all the different aspects of your life. You will instantly notice a "lighter" vibration. Imagine how effective you could be if you were always, or mostly, in this vibration...

Some might think gratitude is just being thankful for the good things in your life. But it's much more than that. It's about being grateful for the tough times *as well as* the good times. Without the tough times, you wouldn't be as strong or resilient as you are today, nor would you have learned the lessons you needed to learn. If you can start seeing things you don't like as "**contrast**," you will discover how you can even be grateful for *them* - because they will point you to what you do want.

You've already started a gratitude journal - well, keep it up until it becomes second nature to you - until you find yourself constantly in an attitude of gratitude.

It's that easy. If you walk away with ONE thing from this book, let it be **gratitude**. Be grateful for anything and everything, and watch it transform your life.

THE STRANGE EXCEPTION

Oddly enough, I have found some benefits in getting mad or angry (!!!).

Don't jump to conclusions. Read this next part carefully...

It is **not** good to get mad at yourself. And it is typically **not** healthy to get angry with others or situations. However, anger can sometimes be a good motivator *if you are directing it toward a state of being that doesn't serve you.*

Let's use addiction, for example. If you are addicted to junk food or cigarettes, you'll notice that they begin to have control over you. In this case, firing yourself up and getting mad at the *control* can leverage the motivation to overcome it. Look at what these things do to you: cost money, create dependency, add excess weight, and take over your mind, for starters. Get angry about *that.*

You can get mad at the state of being unappreciative, knowing this condition isn't working for your well-being. Or you can get angry at your habit of staying up late, knowing that you deserve more sleep.

Just remember: it is crucial that you separate the **state**, or way of thinking, from the REAL you. Don't be mad at YOURSELF for these things - they are human tendencies. You should be doing the opposite and *loving* yourself - getting angry would only be used to discard old, bad habits.

This may not work for you if you find yourself taking it personally. Just view it as another potential life hack for your tool kit.

FAILURE DOESN'T SCARE ME

"Don't fear failure. Not failure, but low aim, is the crime. In great attempts it is glorious even to fail."

— BRUCE LEE

Failure is actually a critical step in achieving goals (we're still getting to goals...). All the greats have failed first, over and over. To overcome the mental blockade of failure, we need to start seeing it differently - as a way to learn and grow. You can't get better without failing, sometimes.

The key, again, is not taking it personally: failure is simply a *feedback mechanism telling you what doesn't work*. And once you know what doesn't work, you can adjust and try something else until you find something that does work.

In his book "Psycho-Cybernetics," Maxwell Maltz includes a great section about failure and how we *need* failure to get what we want! If personal development and mastering your mind interests you, read it at some point.

For now, a good analogy to use is that of an airplane. Did you know that a plane is in error/off-course *90%* of the time? That's right, 90%. And yet it still gets to its *exact* destination. How is that possible?

It's possible because the plane constantly makes tiny adjustments along the way - something called "one-degree course correction." Each time the plane strays off course, these adjustments are instantly made to ensure it stays on track.

Furthermore, the "1 in 60" rule is a guideline that experts in air navigation use. The rule says that if a plane is one degree off course, it will miss its target destination by one mile for every 60 miles it flies. In other words, the further a plane flies at one degree off, the further it will end up from its target (Tandem Thinking 2020). The aircraft would inevitably crash if it weren't for these constant minor adjustments.

Failure can come in many forms, whether a bad grade on a test, a missed opportunity, or a feeling that you didn't quite do your best. Learn to apply the airplane analogy and one-degree course correction: whenever you find yourself off track or "fail" at something, don't get stuck on it. Simply make a tiny adjustment and get back on course. Over time, those small adjustments will add up to big results. But this only works when you use the failure mechanism as your *friend*. Allow failure to consume you, and it becomes your worst enemy.

It is also crucial that you keep focused on the big picture. Take a look at these four growth charts as an example:

As you see, all four charts show growth - although in different ways. By focusing on every failure, you're essentially looking at the "small picture." It's like zooming in on one section of your life through a microscope. This can make every "dip" or "flat" area of the graph seem very overwhelming. But look at the *big* picture, and you'll see that you are going UP - that by trusting in yourself and following your instincts, you are getting to exactly where you want to be. The takeaway: success and growth are **not** straight lines!

I know it can be hard to just "accept" failure, specifically at a young age. It can take many years to learn how to see it for what it *really* is. So let me fill you in on the truth **now**: the truth is that failure is a stepping stone. The truth is that each moment is just a *building block* to the next, better moment. Each "problem" is actually the gateway to your next level of greatness. And everything you overcome expands you.

I challenge you to be wiser than the rest and let failure become your friend - your "friend who is guiding you" to exactly where and who you want to be.

LIVE BOLD AND BRAVE: THE POWER OF SELF-CONFIDENCE

What will self-confidence do for you? Well, for starters, it will give you the power to do things you never thought possible. It will help you take risks and explore new territory. It will provide you with the strength to face challenges head-on. And it will result in a life that is more exciting and fulfilling.

Want to know another remarkable effect of self-confidence? It makes you *attractive* - inside AND out. People are naturally drawn to those who carry themselves with confidence. They see it as a sign of strength, security, and leadership. Don't be surprised when everyone suddenly wants to be around you.

Lastly, you'll be relieved by how self-confidence shakes the imaginary hold that others have on you and the need to rely on what others think of you. In many senses, you will now be completely free.

So - the world is your oyster. Life is your playground. What will you do?

I urge you to live boldly and bravely. Don't let fear hold you back from all life has to offer. You have the power to do great things, so go out there and do them! We live in a time when it's easier and more acceptable than *ever* to be yourself. Don't take this for granted - it certainly wasn't always this way (another thing you can be grateful for)!

Life is limitless, and your newfound self-confidence is your passport to travel. Even as I write this, I am reminded of the continual effects of self-confidence. If you had told me a year ago that I would be an author, I would've told you you're crazy.

Too many people live inside a tiny box of self-imposed restrictions and beliefs. This is nothing more than a shell of a life. Express yourself fully, and push the boundaries. **Remember to balance that with humility and respect for *all* - and you've become unstoppable.**

YOU'VE REACHED THE GOAL(S)!

I couldn't resist one more VERY powerful life hack.

Growing up, I didn't particularly enjoy goal setting. I think I associated the word "goal" with "work." Consequently, as soon as I found myself starting any goal, I also found myself resenting and dropping it. Maybe you're not like me, but thinking about the road ahead and all the "hows" leading up to the end usually burned me out before I even started.

Also, if you notice, I didn't go too deeply into goals at *all* in this book. Maybe that's me channeling my younger self, or perhaps it's just because I *now* know that achieving goals is super easy...

Right now, I'm going to tell you how to effortlessly and powerfully conquer ANY goal - big or small. Ready?

Live like you already have what you want.

Neville Goddard calls this "living in the end" or "living in the wish fulfilled." Essentially, you are putting yourself into the "feeling state" of having already achieved your goal.

> *Example 1*: As I was learning to play guitar, I used this technique and didn't even know it. See, I *rarely* had thoughts like "Ugh, tomorrow I have to learn the A minor scale" or "This week I need to practice stretching my hands so I can play 'Stairway to Heaven,' " etc. Sure, I did those things. But they came naturally, in the moment, due to living in my **desired state**. And what was my desired state? It was something along the lines of: "I'm going to be - no, I AM - a rock star." "I am an amazing musician and performer." "We have the coolest band ever." "We're sharing the stage with *insert fav bands*." "Everybody loves us." Most importantly, I *felt* this way every day.

So, what happened to the "hows"? Well, here's the best part about all of this: **your subconscious mind runs the show**.

The "subconscious mind" is one of my favorite topics; in fact, the immense power of the subconscious still baffles the most brilliant minds today. Perhaps in another book, I will dive deep into this fascinating subject. But for our purposes here, and in closing out this final chapter, know this:

> Your subconscious mind is infinitely more powerful, and intelligent, than your conscious mind. As long as you direct it by telling it "WHAT," it will tackle every "HOW?" with ease.

Yes, by "living in the end," you will *still* be taking action - but it will be **inspired** action, not forced action. The "work" won't even feel like work. It will feel natural – but know that your subconscious mind will be magically on the job behind the scenes.

Example 2: In writing this book, I used this technique again - but this time on purpose. As I said, I never dreamed I would or *could* be an author. But I knew I wanted to write this book. So, I lived in the end: "I am now a successful author." "I am able to help so many people!" "It feels great having my first book out...what's my second book going to be about?" I embedded things like this into my subconscious mind for a few weeks. Very quickly, I had a title. Then, a rough outline. Eventually, the chapters turned into their own little outlines. It just handled itself. And when I wrote, I didn't stress or think about all the things I DIDN'T know (and there were a LOT). I just lived by assuming, by *knowing* that it was already done.

This is just a crash course, but I hope it helps you. Start by practicing with small goals, and you will soon begin proving to yourself what's possible. Then, start pushing the boundaries.

It will take some practice because most of us are taught that achieving great things *needs to be hard*. But I'll tell you what - combine the new, self-confident YOU with a few **bold** goals, and I have a feeling you'll do just fine.

THE NEW MINDSET

This chapter is your victory lap. You've done the work, changed your lens, and now it's time to live in the power of your new mindset—confident, intentional, and **unstoppable**.

🎓 WHAT'S ONE MOMENT FROM YOUR JOURNEY THAT YOU'RE PROUD OF?

Describe what's changed in you.

_____

_____

_____

_____

_____

_____

_____

_____

_____

WHAT IS ONE (OR MORE!) OLD BELIEF OR HABIT YOU'VE COMPLETELY OUTGROWN?

_____

_____

_____

_____

_____

_____

_____

_____

_____

_____

WHAT DOES "FAILURE" MEAN TO YOU NOW?

How can you treat it like a friend instead of a threat?

_____

_____

_____

_____

_____

_____

_____

_____

_____

🔑 HOW CAN ATTITUDE AND GRATITUDE CONTINUE TO SHAPE YOUR LIFE MOVING FORWARD?

_____

_____

_____

_____

_____

_____

_____

_____

_____

_____

✴ WHAT'S SOMETHING BOLD YOU'RE GOING TO DO DIFFERENTLY FROM NOW ON—NO MATTER WHAT ANYONE ELSE SAYS?

_____

_____

_____

_____

_____

_____

_____

_____

_____

THE 9 GOALS CHALLENGE

Write these goals as if they're already true. Think it. Feel it. Act like it.

3 Small Goals

1. _____

2. _____

3. _____

3 Medium Goals

1. _____

2. _____

3. _____

◈ 3 Bold/Big Goals

1. _____

2. _____

3. _____

CONCLUSION: BE THE LIGHT

I thought for a long while about this "conclusion." Now that you are so magnetic, limitless, and powerfully confident, what else could I leave you with? I'm sure the student has become the teacher by this point and that I could probably learn a thing or two from YOU! Even so, here is what finally came to me:

Everyone has the option to use their power for good or for evil. And as you use yours for good (which I know you will), remember that you don't have to *fight* or resist evil to dissolve it.

This is why I ask you to *be the light*.

Light dissolves all shadow. What happens when you walk into a dark room and want it brighter? Do you start punching and kicking the darkness? Do you challenge it to an arm-wrestling competition or call it names? (By the way, if you do - I want to see a video of that.)

No. You simply *turn on the light*.

It's the same way in this world. You must **be** the things you love rather than oppose the stuff you don't love. "What you resist persists." There is no shortage of love, positivity, potential, or "light." It only grows *through* you, as the nature of reality is to expand. Like a candle lighting another candle, your light and love will never "run out." This is the **only** way to illuminate the world.

The journey of life never stops. I urge you to persist in exploring, expanding, discovering, and becoming the best version of yourself possible. Persist in your desire, and persist in your practice. And please - have patience with yourself. Nothing truly worthwhile happens overnight. Nothing great is ever achieved without persistence and patience.

Stay humble. You don't know it all, and you never will. No one likes a know-it-all, anyways. Stay curious. Be open to learning; be open to growing.

But I will say this - if you don't use your power of decision, others will use it for you. And then, *who knows* what kind of hands it will fall into. Hold your power close to your heart, cherish it, and treat it like gold.

Feel free to reread this book or certain sections as often as possible. And by all means - share it and pass it along to others! That's a great way to spread the light.

Alright, good pep talk. Go have fun!

⚒ THE CONFIDENCE TOOLKIT

This section includes bonus pages you can print, re-use, and turn to anytime you need a confidence boost.

🖨 Want printable versions?
Scan the QR code below or visit:

https://qrco.de/confidencetoolkit

CONFIDENCE JOURNAL TEMPLATES

Use these pages to track your progress, release your thoughts, and build deeper self-awareness.

You can write in this book or print copies at https://qrco.de/confidencetoolkit

TODAY I'M PROUD OF...

_____

_____

_____

_____

_____

_____

_____

_____

_____

ONE CHALLENGE I FACED TODAY—AND HOW I HANDLED IT:

_____

_____

_____

_____

_____

_____

_____

_____

_____

♥ SOMETHING I WISH I BELIEVED MORE FULLY ABOUT MYSELF:

_____

_____

_____

_____

_____

_____

_____

_____

_____

◎ A SMALL WIN OR ACT OF COURAGE I NOTICED:

_____

_____

_____

_____

_____

_____

_____

_____

_____

WHAT I'M STILL LEARNING TO ACCEPT ABOUT WHO I AM:

_____

_____

_____

_____

_____

_____

_____

_____

_____

ⅲ MOOD + MINDSET TRACKER

Track your week with these quick prompts. Each day gives you space to capture your mood, thoughts, and a takeaway. Use this to spot patterns and practice emotional awareness.

You can write in this book or print copies at https://qrco.de/confidencetoolkit

MONDAY

Mood:

_____

Shaping Thought:

_____

_____

Takeaway or Insight:

_____

_____

_____

📝 TUESDAY

Mood:

_____

Shaping Thought:

_____

_____

Takeaway or Insight:

_____

_____

_____

WEDNESDAY

Mood:

_____

Shaping Thought:

_____

_____

Takeaway or Insight:

_____

_____

_____

THURSDAY

Mood:

_____

Shaping Thought:

_____

_____

Takeaway or Insight:

_____

_____

_____

FRIDAY

Mood:

_____

Shaping Thought:

_____

_____

Takeaway or Insight:

_____

_____

_____

SATURDAY

Mood:

_____

Shaping Thought:

_____

_____

Takeaway or Insight:

_____

_____

_____

🗒 SUNDAY

Mood:

_____

Shaping Thought:

_____

_____

Takeaway or Insight:

_____

_____

_____

CONFIDENCE BUILDER CARDS

These printable cards are designed to help you build real, unshakable confidence — one phrase at a time. Cut them out, hang them up, tape them to your mirror, or carry them in your pocket. The key is to keep these phrases visible and let them remind you who you are — and who you're becoming.

You'll find 5 pages of Confidence Builder Cards in this section. Each card features a bold, powerful phrase. Every phrase was carefully selected to help boost your self-belief, motivation, and courage.

You can print copies at
https://qrco.de/confidencetoolkit

✅ Tip: Print on thick paper or cardstock for extra durability.

📌 The next pages are your Confidence Builder Cards. Let's go!

I CAN DO
ANYTHING

I AM
STRONG

I Have
What It
Takes

I AM
PROUD
OF WHO I AM

I Do *Scary Things* on Purpose

I DESERVE
TO BE
HEARD

I
TRUST
MYSELF

I
SPEAK
UP

MY VOICE
MATTERS

I'm Allowed
to take
up Space

I'm getting
BRAVER
every day

Confidence
is a Skill
AND I'M BUILDING IT

I'm becoming who I want to be

I don't need to be perfect

I SHOW UP EVEN WHEN IT'S HARD

I KNOW WHO I AM

I'm on my own side

I CAN HANDLE THIS

I'M NOT AFRAID TO BE SEEN	I'm Building My Future
I CAN FIGURE IT OUT	MY EFFORT MATTERS
I'm Brave Enough To Begin	I TRUST MY JOURNEY

🆘 IN CASE OF EMERGENCY

Everyone has tough days. This page is here for those moments when your confidence feels low, and you need a quick reset. Use it to reconnect with your strengths, your support system, and your next small step forward.

Keep this page handy and come back to it whenever you need a reminder that you've already made it through a lot — and you will again.

You can write in this book or print copies at https://qrco.de/confidencetoolkit

IN CASE OF EMERGENCY

When you're feeling totally down, use this page to remind yourself of your strength.

＊＊ Things That Help Me Feel Better＊＊

_____

_____

_____

＊＊👥 People I Can Talk To＊＊

_____

_____

_____

＊＊💪 What I've Already Overcome＊＊

_____

_____

_____

** 👣 One Small Step I Can Take Today**

_____

_____

_____

♥ A LETTER TO FUTURE ME

This is your chance to pause, reflect, and speak to the future version of yourself.

Write a letter to who you'll be one year from now. What do you hope you've done? What do you want to remember? What advice would you give yourself?

Take your time. Be honest. And once it's written, consider sealing this page or setting a reminder to read it again one year from today.

You can write in this book or print copies at https://qrco.de/confidencetoolkit

Dear Future Me,

_____

_____

_____

_____

_____

_____

_____

_____

With excitement,

_____

YOU DID IT!

You've reached the *real* end of this workbook — but this isn't just the end of a project. It's a moment to recognize something big: you committed to growing your confidence. You showed up for yourself. You did the work. And that matters.

Confidence isn't something you either have or don't have. It's something you practice. And now you know how to do that. You've built tools, explored your thoughts, and learned how to lift yourself up when things get hard.

You've written truths, set goals, faced fears, and reflected with honesty. You've proven that you're capable of change — and that's the root of all confidence: knowing that you can grow.

So take a breath. Smile. Be proud. Because what you've done here is powerful.

No one else can live your life for you. But you? You're ready to step into it with courage, clarity, and confidence.

REFERENCES

Abuse: What You Need to Know (for Teens) - Nemours KidsHealth. (n.d.). https://kidshealth.org/en/teens/family-abuse.html

Advice for Bully Victims. (n.d.-a). CABCY Singapore. https://www.cabcy.org.sg/advice-for-bully-victims

Advice for Bully Victims. (n.d.-b). CABCY Singapore. https://www.cabcy.org.sg/advice-for-bully-victims

Biography. (n.d.). The American Foundation for the Blind. https://www.afb.org/about-afb/history/helen-keller/biography-and-chronology/biography

Body Image and Self-Esteem (for Teens) - Nemours KidsHealth. (n.d.). https://kidshealth.org/en/teens/body-image.html

Bowden, D. (2021, March 25). *Self Esteem vs Self Confidence - What's the Difference?* Irreverent Gent. https://www.irreverentgent.com/self-esteem-versus-self-confidence-whats-difference/

Bullies May Face Higher Risk of Substance Use in Adulthood. (2021, March 3). Verywell Mind. https://www.verywellmind.com/bullies-may-face-higher-risk-of-substance-use-in-adulthood-5113768

Clark, C. E. (2018, March 9). *Why I hate the phrase "Fake It 'Til You Make It". . . and a few alternatives.* https://www.linkedin.com/pulse/i-hate-phrase-fake-til-you-make-it-heres-why-here-few-clark

Coelho, P. (2014). *The Alchemist: 25th Anniversary Edition* (Anniversary). HarperOne.

Dispenza, J. (2007). *Evolve Your Brain: The Science of Changing Your Mind.* Health Communications, Incorporated.

Dispenza, J. (2019, June 10). *Evolve Your Brain.* Unlimited With Dr Joe Dispenza. https://drjoedispenza.com/blogs/dr-joes-blog/evolve-your-brain

Dumas, J. L. (2021, June 13). *Reverse Your Limiting Beliefs in as Little as 5 Minutes.* Entrepreneurs on Fire With John Lee Dumas. https://www.eofire.com/reverse-your-limiting-beliefs/

Hartman, C. (n.d.). *Loneliness Statistics (2022): By Country, Demographics & More.* The Roots of Loneliness Project. https://www.rootsofloneliness.com/loneliness-statistics

How Body Image Affects Self-Esteem? | MindShift. (2022, March 10). Mind Shift. https://www.mindshiftwellnesscenter.com/how-body-image-affects-self-esteem/

How to Help Teens Find Purpose. (n.d.). Greater Good. https://greatergood.berkeley.edu/article/item/how_to_help_teens_find_purpose

inc.com. (n.d.). https://www.inc.com/business-insider/21-successful-people-who-rebounded-after-getting-fired.html

Keeler, E. (2013, September 18). *J.K. Rowling wants to help poor single moms — she was one, too.* Los Angeles Times. https://www.latimes.com/books/jacketcopy/la-et-jc-jk-rowling-single-mom-20130918-story.html

Kirby, S. (2019, August 1). *Why Is Exercise Important to Teenagers?* LIVESTRONG.COM. https://www.livestrong.com/article/476879-why-is-exercise-important-to-teenagers/

Label, D. T. (2022, January 17). *Top 10 Tips for Overcoming Bullying.* Ditch the Label. https://www.ditchthelabel.org/top-10-tips-for-overcoming-bullying/

Lazic, M. (2022, October 7). *36 Eye-Opening Bullying Statistics.* What to Become. https://whattobecome.com/blog/bullying-statistics/

Life of Angelina Jolie. (n.d.). Angelina Jolie-pitt. https://angelinajolie-pitt.weebly.com/life-of-angelina-jolie.html

Little, B. (2019, March 15). *7 Things You Didn't Know About Stephen Hawking.* HISTORY. https://www.history.com/news/7-things-you-didnt-know-about-stephen-hawking

Marcus Lemonis. (2021, February 17). *Finding Yourself: A Guide to Discovering your True Self.* https://www.marcuslemonis.com/life-skills/discover-your-true-self

Mimaroglu, A. (2021, January 30). *5 Lessons From the Life of Oprah*. Entrepreneur. https://www.entrepreneur.com/leadership/5-lessons-from-the-life-of-oprah/362598

Monroe, J. (2022a, October 28). *How To Cultivate Positive Teen Body Image*. Newport Academy. https://www.newportacademy.com/resources/well-being/teen-body-image/

Monroe, J. (2022b, October 28). *How To Cultivate Positive Teen Body Image*. Newport Academy. https://www.newportacademy.com/resources/well-being/teen-body-image/

Murphy, J. (2011). *The Power of Your Subconscious Mind*. Martino Publishing.

New Harbinger Publications, Inc. (2020, October 29). *What Is "Guided Journaling" & How Can It Help Anxious Teens?* New Harbinger Publications, Inc. https://www.newharbinger.com/blog/professional/what-is-guided-journaling-how-can-it-help-anxious-teens/

Patel, R. B. (2021, May 12). *Teaching Teens How to Set Healthy Boundaries*. Your Teen Magazine. https://yourteenmag.com/family-life/communication/how-to-set-healthy-boundaries

Psycho-Cybernetics: Updated and Expanded by Maxwell Maltz(2015-03-05). (n.d.). TarcherPerigee.

Rao, C. (2020, March 14). *Was Michael Jordan Really Cut From His High School Basketball Team?* Sportscasting | Pure Sports. https://www.sportscasting.com/was-michael-jordan-really-cut-from-his-high-school-basketball-team/

Robbins, B. A. (2014, September 19). *The Power of Being Different*. Oprah.com. https://www.oprah.com/omagazine/the-power-of-being-different

Rogers, M. (2022, October 3). *What Influences Body Image?* BALANCE Eating Disorder Treatment Center. https://balancedtx.com/blog/what-influences-body-image

Saltz, G., MD. (2022, March 25). *How to Arm Your Child Against Bullying*. Child Mind Institute. https://childmind.org/article/how-to-arm-your-child-against-bullying/

Sigler, K. (2022, August 7). *101 Teen Self Esteem Statistics: Facts We Cannot Ignore in 2022 [infographics]*. SALT Effect. https://www.salteffect.com/teen-self-esteem-statistics/

Singh, A. A. (2020, October 13). *The Mystery And Science Behind The Law Of Attraction*. Forbes. https://www.forbes.com/sites/forbescoachescouncil/2020/10/13/the-mystery-and-science-behind-the-law-of-attraction/?sh=d46dc701a55f

Staff, E. (2022, May 25). *Apple's Steve Jobs: An Extraordinary Career*. Entrepreneur. https://www.entrepreneur.com/growing-a-business/who-was-steve-jobs-see-the-apple-founders-career-and-more/197538

Staff, K. A. W. (2016, March 18). *Love Me Do: Management Lessons from the Fifth Beatle*. Knowledge at Wharton. https://knowledge.wharton.upenn.edu/article/love-management-lessons-fifth-beatle/

Tandem Financial. (n.d.). https://tandemfinancial.co.uk/tandem-thinking/the-power-of-one-degree-course-correction/

Team, S. (2022, October 15). *34 Body Image Statistics You Cannot Afford To Miss (2022)*. Soocial. https://www.soocial.com/body-image-statistics/

The Role of Social Media Influencers in the Lives of Children and Adolescents. (n.d.). Frontiers. https://www.frontiersin.org/research-topics/9295/the-role-of-social-media-influencers-in-the-lives-of-children-and-adolescents

Well, T. (2022, October 4). *What the Mirror Can Teach You About Yourself: Advice from a Mirror Gazing Expert*. Mindful. https://www.mindful.org/what-the-mirror-can-teach-you-about-yourself-advice-from-a-mirror-gazing-expert/

What is bullying? | preventingbullying.promoteprevent.org. (n.d.). http://preventingbullying.promoteprevent.org/what-bullying

What Teens Need to Know About Boundaries. (2021, July 27). Verywell Family. https://www.verywellfamily.com/boundaries-what-every-teen-needs-to-know-5119428

Why teens feel lonely and disconnected | ConnecTeen. (2017, July 25). ConnecTeen | Need Help? 403.264.8336 | Text: 587.333.2724. https://calgaryconnecteen.com/why-teens-feel-lonely-and-disconnected-sometimes/